Endor

Since reading *Everyday Angels* I've had the exciting experience of seeing angels everywhere I go. Even more exciting than that, I have learned to co-labor with them. I've seen miracles as I've asked my co-laborers (angels) to bring God's conviction and healing to those who were not with me.

I'm still learning, but *Everyday Angels* has systematically disassembled many of the misconceptions I grew up with regarding angels. Most of my theology has come from things I've heard people say. In fact, to be honest, all of my theology about angels was hearsay. I never did due diligence to study the matter out for myself. Charity and Joe have done a lot of the work for us and I commend their book as a worthy read for rethinking your concepts of relating to angels.

The proof is in the fruit and I can attest to a greater sense of living in the Spirit and seeing miracles since I've read their book. Take the time to carefully read it for yourself and draw your own conclusions.

TIM MADDEN
YWAM Crossroads DTS Leader
University of the Nations
Kona, Hawaii

I always love the spiritual wisdom Charity Kayembe has to share in her books. *Everyday Angels* is no exception. The partnership between authors, Kayembe and Brock, is delightful. It was interesting to hear both of their perspectives and personal stories. They are so right: the Bible is full of examples of angelic encounters, and there is no reason to believe those stopped or aren't for us today.

I loved Kayembe's reminder that our angels are always with us; it doesn't just have to be a special visitation or a one-time encounter. Brock and Kayembe have opened my eyes on what to look for. The idea that angels have assigned tasks related to us is fascinating as well. As Brock reminds us, "Jesus was ministered to by angels, and we are to be ministered to by them as well."

CHERYL MCKAY
Screenwriter, *The Ultimate Gift*
Co-writer of feature films, *Extraordinary and Indivisible*
Author, *Finally the Bride: Finding Hope While Waiting*
Co-author, *Never the Bride*

I love *Everyday Angels!* This book excited me as I read the testimonies and scriptural accounts. As a result, I have a fresh hunger for more encounters with God, His truth, and His ways. For some, this book will stretch and challenge you but it will surely impact all who read it!

DR. PATRICIA KING
Founder Patricia King Ministries
www.patriciaking.com

In *Everyday Angels*, Charity Virkler Kayembe and Joe Brock offer an intriguing exploratory look into the world of angels in the everyday lives of believers. The duo describes personal angelic encounters and offers practical, biblical teaching on what they call the "rules of engagement." If you are hungry for new perspectives on the angelic realm, read this book cover to cover and build your faith for angelic perception.

JENNIFER LECLAIRE
Senior Leader, Awakening House of Prayer
Founder, Ignite Prophetic Network

Everyday Angels by Charity Virkler Kayembe and Joe Brock offers an excellent biblical and experiential summary of "everyday" angelic activity that most Christians scarcely notice. As a three year-old, I fell into a flood stage river and was drowning, but was rescued by what I described as an angel. A lady in our church who knew nothing of this had been desperately interceding for me all that morning. So I am here today to verify the theme of what Charity and Joe have written!

Everyday Angels is an eye-opener to the amazing warrior-helpers God has provided His beloved children who think they are alone and helpless.

JON RUTHVEN, PhD
Director, Iris University PhD Program
Author, *What's Wrong with Protestant Theology* and
On the Cessation of the Charismata

When you finally find the perfect biblically sound book about angels, a book that is full of personal angel stories—and when that book features a Foreword written by Joshua Mills—you know you've just discovered gold!

Such is the case of this book, *Everyday Angels*. People are often afraid of angel stories for fear of being accused of dabbling in the New Age. But this is *not* that kind of book. On the contrary, this book is the real thing, including showing you how to have a personal friendship relationship with your angels. Can somebody shout "Yes, Lord!"

This isn't one of those works that would help you just a little bit. This is a book that is under that special category called, "Books you *must have*." Please, get one and buy one for a friend too!

STEVE SHULTZ
Founder, The Elijah List

Everyday Angels by Charity Virkler Kayembe and Joe Brock will certainly capture the reader with the reality of the powerful relationship we can experience on a daily basis with God's angels. Biblically sound, this book heralds the wondrous and relatively unexplored frontier of angelic partnership that all believers in Christ can experience.

MARIE CHAPIAN, PhD
Author of *Angels in Our Lives*

DESTINY IMAGE BOOKS
BY CHARITY VIRKLER KAYEMBE

Unleashing Healing Power Through Spirit-Born Emotions (with Mark Virkler)

Hearing God Through Your Dreams (with Mark Virkler)

everyday
angels

How to Encounter, Experience,
and Engage Angels in Everyday Life

CHARITY VIRKLER KAYEMBE
AND JOE BROCK

DESTINY IMAGE® PUBLISHERS, INC.

P.O. Box 310, Shippensburg, PA 17257-0310

"Promoting Inspired Lives."

This book and all other Destiny Image and Destiny Image Fiction books are available at Christian bookstores and distributors worldwide.

Cover design by Eileen Rockwell

Interior design by Terry Clifton

For more information on foreign distributors, call 717-532-3040.

Reach us on the Internet: www.destinyimage.com.

ISBN 13 TP: 978-0-7684-4275-5

ISBN 13 eBook: 978-0-7684-4276-2

ISBN 13 HC: 978-0-7684-4278-6

ISBN 13 LP: 978-0-7684-4277-9

For Worldwide Distribution, Printed in the U.S.A.

4 5 6 7 8 / 22 21

Charity's Dedication

To Jasmine, Rebekah and Hudson.
I love you to the moon and back!
—Auntie Charity

Joe's Dedication

I want to dedicate this book first and foremost to My Lord.
All of this is possible because of You and You alone.
Thanks for being such a great Friend.
Secondly, to my wife and kids
—Holly, Hannah, Joshua, Charis, Chloe and Sophie—
you are my favorite people in the world.
Love you all.

Acknowledgments

We are grateful to all the amazing people we have met who shared their angel stories with us and allowed us to include them in this book. We know so many will be encouraged by your incredible testimonies. You are an inspiration!

We also want to thank the awesome publishing team at Destiny Image. Larry, John, Brad, Meelika, Wil, and Cavet—you are a pleasure to work with and we so appreciate your diligence and commitment to excellence. Bless you!

Joe also wishes to thank...

I want to acknowledge Dr. Charity Virkler Kayembe and Dr. Mark Virkler. Thank you for giving me this opportunity and for all your help in the development of this book. May it be used by the Lord to change lives and destinies.

Contents

Foreword

by Joshua Mills

I believe with all my heart that God wants to pour out a heavenly blessing in this day that will release the reality of His Glory Realms around us. Within those realms, He will introduce us to the supernatural dimension of the angelic and their compelling purpose for interacting within our lives.

Throughout the Scriptures we are encouraged to seek first the Kingdom realities of God. This means positioning ourselves for an understanding and revelation of the heavens. Throughout recorded history there has been miraculous angelic intervention among mankind. God's ways are unchanging and His methods for pouring out His glory remain the same: He chooses to use angels along with willing vessels in order to release His blessings on the earth.

In our lives, my wife Janet and I have experienced a lot of angelic encounters in our home and in our ministry. And we know that such encounters are not only for us but for everyone. These Glory Realms are opening—not just for the older ones but for the younger ones. Not just for the younger ones but for the older ones. These Glory Realms are opening for everyone today—it's for the entire body of Christ to walk in and begin experiencing the divine supernatural together. That is why I am so excited about this important book.

Interestingly enough, I first met Charity when we were both part of a short-term mission's trip as teenagers. We became good friends and pen pals after we returned home. We lost touch over the years, and the Lord continued to work in both of our lives. Then, last fall, our paths suddenly crossed again when we were both ministering in some of the same churches throughout Europe. We reconnected and the Lord is again building strong bonds of friendship. So I was honored when she asked me to write a Foreword to her newest book on angels.

I love this book, because I believe in the validity of its message and I know that you will discover an impartation as you read the testimonies and the unfolding revelation. Janet and I could feel the presence of the Lord as we read through it page by page, and at times, we had to pause our reading in order to enjoy the encounter that God was bringing us into. I encourage you to do the same, as you enjoy both the written word and the spirit of this book.

Like Charity, I first encountered angels as a young child. While playing around the house or in the yard, there were spirit beings that I interacted with. My parents called them my "imaginary friends" because no one else could see them, but they were real to me. They played with me and they were my real friends. At church, another little girl and I would enjoy watching the angels flying around the sanctuary during worship.

Unfortunately, one of the adults overheard us talking about them and scolded us for making up stories and lying. "You can't see angels," they said. "They don't fly around the church." At that moment my child-like faith was stolen and that realm was shut down for me. I didn't see angels again until much later in my life.

One night, in a dream, the Lord re-introduced me to this angelic realm and the three specific angels who are assigned to me. I learned their names and their ministry functions in my life. Like Charity's angels, they appeared as men like me, only bigger, taller, stronger and more powerful. Since that night, angels have been an important part of my life and ministry. I thank God that He has given His angels charge over us, that He has assigned His angels as messengers and servants to bring His purposes to the earth and in our lives.

God is still watching over His Word to perform it, and one of the ways He is doing it is through His ministry of angels. You will read several exciting accounts in Joe's chapters of this book in which he shares some of his intercessory journeys where he was directed by the Lord to partner with angels to accomplish His purposes. Something I have learned is, there is always more to see in God. It doesn't matter how much supernatural experience we've had in the past, God always wants to show us something new.

I've noticed a recent shift in the atmosphere, and it's causing a greater flow of angelic activity within the earth than ever before. For that reason, I've begun teaching an 'Angel School' in various places around the world, because there is a moment of invitation that the Spirit of God is inviting us into. It is the cooperation of Heaven and earth, to bring forth God's end-time purposes before the soon coming of Jesus Christ. We must become well-acquainted with these heavenly helpers.

I believe that this book has the ability to open you up to exciting new encounters within this heavenly realm, giving you scriptural guidelines and modern-day examples to follow! Charity and Joe will answer, biblically and authoritatively, just about any question you might have about angelic encounters, such as: Doesn't interacting with angels detract from our relationship with Jesus? Why do we need angels if we have the Holy Spirit in us, on us, and with us? What about worshiping angels and satan as an angel of light? Aren't we going to be deceived?

You will read many of God's personal directives to Charity, re-introducing her to her angelic bodyguards and encouraging them to be friends. You will enjoy several of the conversations she has had with her angels, demonstrating their surprisingly fun and funny personalities as the relational beings God created.

Like Zechariah and Daniel, Jesus in the Gospels and John in Revelation, you will join with the angels God has assigned to partner with you to disciple nations and bring Heaven to earth. With strong biblical safeguards, you will be led step by step into the divine super-natural for yourself, activating you into your own personal experiences with the company of Heaven.

When God wants to send us a visitation in this day of the angelic realm from the Glory Realms of Heaven, we need to receive that which God is releasing. If God wants to send down angelic encounter, if God wants to release miracles, if God wants to release supernatural won-ders—if He wants to release the essence of His Kingdom and His Presence—we need to receive what He is doing in this day because it is so big—it is so large—it is beyond that which we can contain.

I highly encourage you to read this book, as you open your mind and your heart to become acquainted with the *Everyday Angels* that God has given to you!

JOSHUA MILLS
International Glory Ministries
Palm Springs, California
www.joshuamills.com

Preface

By Dr. Mark Virkler

The Bible is meant to be LIVED! The Scriptures were not given just to be a record of the lives of believers in the past but to show us how we can live today. The supernatural was clearly in the center of the relationship between the biblical saints and the Lord, and it should not be unknown or frightening to us. We are supposed to interact and engage with the spiritual realm as a normal part of our everyday lives.

In this outstanding book, Charity and Joe clearly teach you how to develop that lifestyle. As they so plainly demonstrate, the spirit world should not be visitational but habitational.

Christianity is not like every other religion that is limited to rules, laws, ceremonies and traditions. We cannot claim biblical Christianity if it can be experienced through just our own efforts. Everything about our faith declares that it is supernatural. Our salvation experience itself was a supernatural event where the spirit realm broke into our mundane physical existence. For me, it was prompted by a recurring, flowing thought, telling me I needed to be prepared for eternity. That "thought" was from God. I honored it and I was born again, from above. So I began my Christian experience by the Spirit.

Now, having been born of the Spirit, we don't want to fall back into a limited material lifestyle. Rather, we want to press on to maturity in our spiritual life. We are called to live by the Spirit, walk by the Spirit, seek the things that are above, look at what is not seen (see Gal. 5:25; Col. 3:2; 2 Cor. 4:18). We are born again to live in and see and hear the spirit realm as normally and naturally as we live in and see and hear the physical world. We are born from above and supernatural living is our birthright.

The Bible is our model, and it shows us that the way to Christian maturity is to immerse ourselves in the voice of God, visions from God, angelic encounter, dreams, the gifts of the Spirit and other supernatural experiences. We can trust the Holy Spirit to be our Guide and depend on the Scriptures as our roadmap to fearlessly explore the spirit realm. The mature, through practice, have their senses trained to discern good and evil (see Heb. 5:14). That is how we grow up in spiritual things: we practice. The more we practice interacting with the sacred supernatural, the safer, stronger and wiser we will be, and the easier it will be to distinguish satan's counterfeit from the divine.

It is time for the Church to stop being surprised or impressed or frightened when a believer confidently engages the sacred supernatural. Indeed, we should be shocked to meet one who is a committed follower of Christ who does not interact with the spirit world as a normal part of their daily lives. Our journey of faith is to be vibrant, filled with living encounter with the living God. The alternative is to live by regulations and reasoning about Him. Instead, God invites us to live *with* Him, in

His realm of the spirit, with His heavenly hosts. The writer of Hebrews declares that we *have come* to the city of the living God, the heavenly Jerusalem and to myriads of angels (see Heb. 12:22)!

If we seek the Kingdom of Heaven, we will meet not only the Father, Jesus and the Holy Spirit. We will encounter the hosts of Heaven—the angel armies, the angel messengers, the angel guardians and the angels worshiping. There is no reason to fear interacting with these spirit beings for God identifies with them when He calls Himself the "Lord of Hosts," that is, the Lord of the Armies of Heaven. They are under His authority, and when we are speaking His word and His will, they are under our authority as well.

Angels are an integral part of the Kingdom that we now inhabit. The Lord has given His angels as ministering servants to His children (see Heb. 1:14). Why would we ignore or rudely command these glorious creations whose joy it is to serve us? Why wouldn't we interact with them and get to know them, receive their messages, and partner with them?

Is it safe? Well, what is it that keeps me safe? The Lord spoke into my heart, "Mark, you can trust My voice in your heart, more than you can trust the reasoned theology of your mind." Really! I explained to the Lord that I had an evil and desperately wicked heart, so how could I possibly trust a voice coming from it. I even had Scripture to prove I had an evil heart—Jeremiah 17:9.

Jesus' response back was, "I have given you a new heart and put a new spirit within you" (Ezek. 36:26-27). He went on to say that since I have been born again, I no longer have an evil heart but I was now a partaker of the divine nature (see 2 Pet. 1:4) and I could trust the flow of His Spirit within (see Jn. 7:37-39) more than I could trust the reasoning of my mind.

Wow! Talk about a transformation in my life. I now choose to live heart first, rather than head first. I have decided that safety comes, not from my ever-changing theology, but through a multitude of Spirit-led counselors (see Prov. 11:14), as well as the other biblical parameters that Charity clearly lays out. If you will follow the path she shows you, you can confidently enter the heavenly realm.

Everyday Angels invites you into supernatural Christianity. Charity and Joe take you by the hand to lead you there safely. There are guardrails along the path so you needn't be afraid. Step into your destiny as a supernatural child of God, born of the Spirit, whose citizenship is in Heaven!

Prologue

by Charity Kayembe

I grew up in supernatural Christianity. My parents named their ministry "Communion with God" and they have invested their lives in empowering believers to live out of their conversational relationship with Jesus every day. With a foundation like that, it's no surprise that I live for scriptural, mystical encounter. The Bible is not a book of old stories. It is a model for what our lives can look like right now.

In Scripture, we see that God uses angels to direct, encourage, protect, and instruct His people. Just like He uses dreams to bless us, God uses angels in our lives. And far from being random occurrences that happen once or twice in our lifetimes, angelic intervention is, in fact, God's *modus operandi*. He created angels. God Himself designed the spiritual landscape to include angels—it was His original intention.

We usually think of angels appearing in our church services, and that is great. We may see them during our worship times or prayer meetings. Praise God! We are so thankful for these ministering spirits caring for us who have inherited salvation (see Heb. 1:14).

However, most of us don't spend our entire lives in church. We go to work. We attend school. We enjoy time with our families at home. Are angels with us then? Surely it is *outside* the four walls of the church that we need them most!

So, what would that look like? We have been blessed by testimonies of angels in our meetings on Sunday morning, but where are they on Monday morning in our office building? Or on Saturday morning when we are at the gym?

We want to take our Christianity outside of our church services and live the Bible every day, in our everyday lives. If we engage the supernatural and expect to follow scriptural examples of angelic encounter and assistance—what does that actually look like?

That is what we are going to spend the rest of this book exploring. Two of my best friends are my angelic guardians. I have seen them since I was a little girl, and they are always with me. We all have angels assigned to us, and I want to share my story with you so you too can step into the sacred supernatural and live to that unseen world.

Jesus taught that this spiritual realm is called Heaven and I invite you to accompany me on a journey to further explore this holy Kingdom. There are angels there and they are on your side. They are fun, and funny! And they can't wait to meet you.

Who We Are

I am grateful for my co-author Pastor Joe Brock and the similarities we share. Like me, he was a preacher's kid. We both grew up in church, attended Bible School, and now we are active in ministry. And although we don't see angels all the time, we do see angels whenever we look for them.

Joe is a devout student of the Word and well versed in Scripture and in the original languages in which Scripture was written. His insights into the Greek and Hebrew will not only bless you but also give you a deeper foundation in the Bible so you may soar even more freely in the heights of the Spirit.

I also appreciate what Joe and I don't have in common. While we both have prolific experiences with the angelic realm, you will immediately notice how different those experiences are. Our purpose is to demonstrate some of the many different ways you can potentially partner with the company of Heaven.

What is it like to work with angels and do life together with them? The answer is as varied as there are people on earth. Just like us, angels have been fashioned with different personalities and functions within the Kingdom.

For example, unlike me, Joe shares some dramatic stories of spiritual warfare and even international exploits with his heavenly battalion! I know you will be encouraged and inspired by his testimonies to see all that is available in your own supernatural walk in the Spirit.

But Isn't This New Age?

Some of what we share may sound New Age to you. However, Titus 1:15 tells us that "to the pure all things are pure." So when Joe and I talk about interacting with angels, that does not sound New Age to us at all. Instead, it sounds like Zechariah. It sounds like Daniel. It sounds like Jesus in the Gospels and John in the book of Revelation.

I am not really familiar with the New Age Movement or what New Age followers believe. I do know they have books and even classes on angels, but I have never read those books or attended the classes, so I am not aware of what they teach.

And I prefer it that way.

I actually take it as a wonderful confirmation that unbelievers are counterfeiting the truth that I live in. That shows that what I am experiencing is authentic and valuable. Nobody counterfeits $1.00 bills. They only counterfeit what has great worth.

Also, it is significant that there are no counterfeit $3.00 bills either. Why is that? Because in the United States there are no real, legal $3.00 bills. Therefore, the fact that the New Age is counterfeiting angelic experience proves two things: angels are real and interacting with them has value.

Instead of studying other faiths, I just stick to reading my Bible. There are over three hundred verses on angels found there, which is more than enough to offer a strong scriptural foundation and precedent for my own angelic experiences.

It is interesting to note how banks train tellers to recognize counterfeit currency. They do not have them study fake money or examine counterfeit bills. They do the opposite. They simply have them focus on legal tender, the legitimate, true bills. As a result, they are so familiar with the authentic that they immediately recognize anything that is not genuine.

So it is with our supernatural experiences.

We want to focus intently on the Word of God, the Bible. We want to be so thoroughly familiar with what God Himself has said about angels, with how He has used them in the lives of His children for millennia, and how He's shown us in the book of Revelation that He will continue to use them in the future, that we don't doubt it anymore. We understand Father's heart and His intention for angels to bless us, to minister to us, to help us.

But how can angels do that when we are afraid to interact with them? The New Age did not invent angels. God is the one who imagined angels, created them each individually, and assigned them to us. They are God's idea.

There Is More!

What I love so much about New Agers is that they are hungry for the supernatural. In fact, that is one of the reasons I wrote this book. I was asked for recommendations for books on angels from a biblical perspective, since much of what is available on interacting with angels has been written by those within the New Age Movement.

I appreciate that New Agers realize there is more. They are right! We were never designed to be limited by this four-dimensional space-time matrix. We are spirit beings, created in the image of our heavenly Father, who is Spirit (see John 4:24). God's original intention was for us to live with Him, and live like Him.

In summary, just because there are counterfeit bills in the world does not mean we run away from cash, afraid that what we have may not be the real deal. In the same way, just because people of other faiths are doing similar things does not mean that we will run away from the real, authentic and "legal" angelic experience that our heavenly Father designed us to have according to Scripture.

The Bible is not a box that we awkwardly cram our lives into. The Bible is a sure foundation that we confidently build our lives upon. By knowing the Word of God intimately and experientially, we are able to venture into the spirit realm safely and strongly, without fear or hesitation. Like Jesus, we will learn to live into the spirit easily, and live out of the supernatural naturally.

This is what we were made for.

Let the journey begin!

Introduction

by Joe Brock

I have to admit I am genuinely excited to write this book with Charity Kayembe for a couple of reasons. First, Charity is a highly enthusiastic lover of God. She pushes the boundaries of her beliefs and allows the Lord to teach her deeper things of the Kingdom.

The second reason is that for years, I have had varying degrees of angelic encounters and have not shared them with a larger audience. Often when I shared an experience, people would try to make me out as something special or unique. This disturbed me greatly. The things of God's Kingdom are for all His kids.

I know we have gifts and callings, but I believe our hunger is the greatest factor in determining what we actually receive. I stopped sharing because I would not let myself be seen as anything more than what I am—someone whom God's grace found and redeemed. God loves us all equally and I fully believe all of us are to be the recipients of His Kingdom. Angels are not for a select few, but for "the sake of those who are to inherit salvation" (Heb. 1:14).

As the future unfolds, days may seem to be growing darker. Fear and trepidation may try to control us. However, God has been speaking to me about all believers increasing their everyday partnership with the angelic realm.

This is why I want to share what I am learning. We are on the same team. Your success is my success and mine is yours. If we can help each other grow in our understanding and then translate this into our daily lives, we will see great days ahead. Angels are all around us and they are waiting for instruction and assignments. As we learn to see and partner with angels, our lives improve dramatically.

Chapter 1

Angels 101: A Biblical Overview

by Charity Kayembe

Angels are God's idea and I am grateful He created them. Angels and I both love God, we have been assigned by Him as co-workers together, and we happily serve Him as a team. However, that wasn't always the case. I started well, got derailed for a minute, but now I do life together with them again.

When I was a little girl, I always talked about my invisible play-mates. While some parents might have wanted their kids to "grow up" and stop telling stories about "imaginary" friends, my parents encouraged it. My mom always believed I was seeing my guardian angels, and my dad always taught me to look at the things that are unseen, because that is the most real reality (see 2 Cor. 4:18).

My angelic guardians introduced themselves to me when I was young, and at four years old I told my mom their names: Pojes and

Shobis (pronounced Poe-jis and Show-bis). Since we are all good friends now, I sometimes just use their nicknames for short, Poje and Shobi (pronounced Poge and Show-bee).

Adventures in Smuggling

I remember seeing my angels with me as I was growing up. For example, when I was on a mission trip and we were carrying Bibles into a closed country, they were right there with me. I had a backpack full of "bread," not to mention pockets bulging with tracts, and I walked right past the security checkpoint and x-ray machines with no detection by the guards. I saw Pojes and Shobis run interference and stand between me and the soldiers, blocking me from their view. The border patrol never stopped me because they never saw me!

Surprisingly though, most of the time I didn't really appreciate what they did. Even though I saw my angels around, I didn't talk with them much. Well, I would talk *at* them and give them orders, because I saw them as only ministering servants sent to help me. While that is true, I was definitely missing something since being dictatorial and having a one-sided relationship does not display the Spirit of Christ.

The problem was, somewhere along the line my beliefs about angels got off track. I somehow developed two wrong ideas which kept me from interacting with them even though I knew they were there. First, I decided it might be disrespectful to Jesus to hang out with my angels. I thought I should focus on Him since He's right here with me. After all, He's God, and angels are not. I don't want to disregard or dishonor Him in any way.

Because I didn't want to overemphasize angels, my solution was to marginalize them and completely ignore the very assistants God had sent to bless and help me.

The other lie I believed was that we no longer need angels now that we are in the New Covenant, have Holy Spirit in us, and have access to God's strength and gifts. What can angels do that God can't? Obviously, nothing. Somehow, I thought I was giving God more credit by not seeing any need for angels; I believed I was doing Him a favor by overlooking their work in my life.

Allow Me to Introduce You

God was not impressed with either of these incorrect beliefs, and He lovingly made that clear the day He re-introduced me to my angels. He said, "Okay guys, you're friends, partners, and co-laborers for and with Me. We're all on the same team! Hang out and chat. Be friendly, and be friends."

(If having a two-way conversation with God is new to you, please refer to Appendix B. Hearing His voice is easier than you think!)

Now I am all for obedience, but I still felt it necessary to explain to God how I was actually trying to be nice to Him by ignoring my angels. I was giving my quiet times exclusively to Him, and wasn't that so sweet and thoughtful of me? While He did appreciate my heart's motivation, He gently enlightened me to His perspective and why I really didn't need to worry about hurting His feelings or insulting Him.

God said, "Remember, I created family. I made Eve for Adam because it wasn't good for him to be alone. I put you in a family with a mom and dad and brother and gave you a husband and friends. So I am the One who created relationships, and put you into them. Lots of them! Interconnected. Family. Members of a body.

"The point is, I'm not threatened by your having other relationships and friendships outside of your fellowship with Me. Why would I be?

I'm not selfish like that. That is the way love is not jealous" (see 1 Cor. 13:4).

Of course. I knew that! God's not insecure. Why did I think He would be so petty? I definitely needed to renew and conform my mind to His. What He said made much more sense than what I had been thinking.

I also realized how inconsistent my beliefs were. I thought I shouldn't talk with angels in order to avoid focusing on them too much. However, many of us (myself included) are already engaging the angelic and simply don't realize it. We know that our enemy, satan, is a fallen angel. We have books, seminars, and entire ministries that are devoted to spiritual warfare, which is essentially angel-focused ministry. We have focused exclusively on the fallen instead of the faithful. To be fair, we should give at least as much attention to God's holy angels as well!

Scriptural Precedents

But I still had another concern: What about Holy Spirit? Why would I need angels since my spirit is connected to God's Spirit? It does not seem like there should be anything missing or lacking in my life or ministry since God Himself is with me and in me. Or is there?

The only way to really know anything for sure is to find out what the Bible says. I quickly discovered it says a whole lot more about angels than I ever noticed before. There are literally hundreds of verses about angels in Scripture. The majority of books mention them, and there are whole chapters devoted to describing angelic encounter such as those in Daniel and Zechariah. If you look at the heroes of the Old Testament, you will see that angels met with many of them: Abraham, Jacob, Moses, David, Elijah, Elisha, Ezekiel and Isaiah, to name just a few.

What I found to be even more incredible were all the New Testament accounts of angels, from Joseph to Mary to Zacharias to Cornelius. Of course, the entire book of Revelation is a record of John's encounter with Jesus and angels. In fact, angels are mentioned more in the New Testament than the Old, even though the New Testament is much shorter.

I still wondered about Holy Spirit though. Were there believers who were filled with Holy Spirit, connected to God and His wisdom and power, who still needed help from angels? I found many accounts of New Testament disciples who did, including Peter (see Acts 5:19; 12:7-11), John (see Rev. 1:1), Philip (see Acts 8:26) and Paul (see Acts 27:23-24).

Father God could have certainly set Peter free from the jail cell all by Himself. Holy Spirit could have told Paul not to worry about the storm and confirmed that the crew would be safe. And Jesus could have easily given John his revelations of Heaven, as He was standing right there and obviously a part of the vision, too (see Rev. 22:16).

Instead, God chose to use angels.

Jesus and Angels

Of course, our ultimate example is Jesus, so what about Him? He *is* God. Surely, I thought, He does not require angelic assistance. Well, it turns out He does—or at least He wants it. It is the way Father set it up: for angels to minister to us (see Heb. 1:13-14).

We know angels prophesied to Mary and then to Joseph about Jesus being born. Angels proclaimed His birth in Bethlehem, and they surrounded His resurrection and later ascension. But what really amazed me was the fact that angels ministered to Jesus in the wilderness (see

Matt. 4:11) and strengthened Him in the Garden of Gethsemane (see Luke 22:43).

Since angels are such important figures in the Bible, in the lives of the disciples, and in the life of Jesus Himself, why shouldn't they be a bigger part of my life?

What Can't They Do?

I had finally accepted the fact that angels can be around, but I still had some pretty specific and limited tasks I understood to be in their repertoire of usefulness. For example, the book of Psalms makes it clear that they can protect me (see Ps. 34:7 and 91:11).

I decided angels could also explain things to me, since that happens repeatedly throughout the Prophets. I learned, though, that they actually do all kinds of other things, too, from making dinner (see 1 Kings 19:5-8) to even playing a role in healing (see John 5:4).

But if there is one thing all Christians would agree on, it is that no angel could have anything to do with cleansing man from sin. Yet the Bible tells us something different.

The sixth chapter of Isaiah makes it crystal clear how important angels are and how much they really can do. Here we find Isaiah having his great vision where he sees the Lord high and lifted up. God is on His throne and there are angels surrounding Him. So far, so good. But look at what happens when Isaiah worries about his sin in the presence of a holy God:

> Then one of the seraphim flew to me with a burning coal in his hand, which he had taken from the altar with tongs. He touched my mouth with it and said, "Behold, this has touched your lips; and your iniquity is taken away and your sin is forgiven" (Isaiah 6:6-7).

God was with Isaiah and certainly could have touched Isaiah's mouth with the coal. "What?" I asked. "God, You were right there! You were with Isaiah. You could have easily done this Yourself. I know it is Jesus' blood and sacrifice that saves us, so why did You let an angel touch him with the burning coal? If I had given this vision, I definitely would have had You get up from Your throne and bring that coal over to Isaiah Yourself. You didn't need an angel to do that for You."

Father's Point of View

God responded, "Of course I didn't *need* an angel to do it. You're right that I don't 'need' anyone to do anything. But I'm God, and I like it this way. I'm a King. I'm on a throne. Why wouldn't I want My servants to serve Me? Why wouldn't I want to commission those under My authority to do the work I want accomplished?

"While you are right about My abilities, I *choose* this way. I *designed* angels to be part of the spiritual landscape. I like them! They like serving Me. It's really a win-win situation. You had been thinking that having servants detracts from My power or awesomeness in some way, but actually the opposite is true.

"Kings and presidents and prime ministers don't do everything for themselves. They don't go out to war personally, do they? They send armies out on their behalf, with their full authority and strength behind them.

"It does not diminish Me to have angelic servants that I work through; it glorifies Me. So when you realize you guys are all on the same team, partnering together to obey Me and serve Me, that thrills Me. That is the vision! That is how it's supposed to work.

"So don't feel the need to question anymore. You have a biblical basis and My personal invitation and instruction—run with it. We can accomplish so much more through unity, with everyone on the same team aware of each other and cooperating together with their teammates. You are not alone and never have been. I never leave you or forsake you, and neither do they. Because they live in perfect obedience to My will, and My will for them is to watch over you" (see Ps. 91:11).

What Are They Like?

Now that I had my big questions answered I could finally enjoy getting to know my angelic bodyguards. So, what are they actually like? They're like the big brother you always wished you had, or the best version of your very best friend. They are authentic and charming, heroic and faithful, unexpectedly fun and funny. Almost like stand-up comedian, buddy comedy movie funny.

I asked, "Are you guys for real?"

Their response: "Fun? I know, not the first thing you usually think of when you consider angelic guardians. We get that a lot."

That's pretty funny! Another morning Shobi complimented me, "If I may say so, Milady, you are a vision..."

Rolling my eyes I laughed at him, "Thanks, and I could certainly say the same thing about YOU" (considering he actually is an invisible spirit from another dimension). He said that just to make me laugh, I know. They do that a lot. They tell me they are "guardians of my laughter" and "protectors of my peace."

One day I tried to turn the tables on them and tease them back. "So about your names. I mean, Pojes and Shobis? Really? No offense, but they're just really not that cool..."

They replied, "Yeah, actually—we're not from around here."

Ha! Well, I certainly couldn't argue with that.

In fact, over the years I have discovered that my angels are just like my husband, in that they love to hear me laugh. Pojes, Shobis and Leo all go out of their way to elicit a smile or laugh from me, just because they want to see me happy and peaceful and in that good place.

God taught me many things through these angelic encounters. One revelation was how laughter is actually a swipe at the enemy. Since satan's strategy is to steal our peace, kill our joy, and bring destruction to us spirit, soul, and body, our laughter is the simplest way to express his total failure in all of those areas. This is one of the reasons why holy laughter has been such a distinctive element of revival.

Peace Keepers

I was excited when I found Bill Johnson shared a similar idea in his book *Hosting the Presence* and took it as confirmation that this was indeed a God thought.

> It's important to note that violence in the spiritual realm is always a peace-filled moment for His people. That's how the Prince of Peace can crush satan under our feet (see Rom. 16:20). Another way to put it is every peace-filled moment you experience brings terror to the powers of darkness. Only in the Kingdom of God is peace a military tool.[1]

Yes! That is exactly what the Lord had been teaching me. But honestly, I still needed to have a talk with Jesus about these angels He assigned to me.

"Jesus, they're really awesome and everything, and I don't mean to sound ungrateful, but they are just so into my feelings (of all things!). Guardians of my joy. Seriously? There has to be more important things for all of us to be concerned with. I mean, isn't there a spiritual war going on? Where are these guys on that anyway?"

Jesus just laughed, obviously amused, and assured me that my angels were obeying Him perfectly and precisely accomplishing the mission He had given them. He then went on to show me how holy emotion was a big player throughout the entire New Testament.

While I already knew about the fruit of the Spirit (love, joy, peace—see Gal. 5:22-23), He also reminded me about the abiding realities of faith, hope and love (see 1 Cor. 13:13). First Corinthians 13 tells us that if we don't have the fruit of the Spirit in our lives then the gifts don't matter. Spiritual gifts (e.g., miracles and prophecy) are to demonstrate the spiritual fruit of God's heart—His feelings of patience, kindness, and compassion toward us.

The most exciting revelation was when He highlighted Romans 14:17. Righteousness, peace, and joy in the Holy Ghost are actually the very Kingdom of God. He could not put a higher premium on them than that. And if that wasn't enough, Holy Spirit then showed me how His Kingdom emotions even play a part in our spiritual warfare.

What Kind of Armor?

First came the understanding that harboring feelings like anger (see Eph. 4:26-27) and unforgiveness can give place to the devil in our lives (see 2 Cor. 2:10-11).

Then, God showed me that from head to toe, we are dressed in His feelings, which guard and protect us. The armor for our spiritual battles is actually made of God's emotions: A breastplate of faith and love, a helmet of hope (see 1 Thess. 5:8), and shoes made of peace (see Eph. 6:15).

I was incredibly blessed when I then came across Pastor Bill's word about peace-filled moments bringing terror to the enemy. Because what is the best outward expression of peace? Laughter sure works for me, which is exactly what my angels had been trying to tell me all along.

If personal revelation, Scripture, and Bill Johnson agree? I must be on the right track!

In fact, even science now confirms the extraordinary health benefits of positive feelings. The Center for Disease Control tells us that up to 75 percent of sickness and disease is caused by stress and the National Council on Compensation of Insurance has found that up to 90 percent of visits to primary care physicians are because of stress-related complaints.[2]

What is the opposite of stress? Peace and joy. If God and His company of Heaven can keep us in a place of experiencing Kingdom emotions, He has just delivered us from 90 percent of illness. No wonder He says His holy emotions protect and guard us![3]

What About You?

- How do you view angels? Have you honored all the Bible teaches about them?

- What is the most helpful insight you took away from this chapter?

- Read Zechariah chapters 1–6. Who explained spiritual things to Zechariah? Did Zechariah ask questions of him, and was that okay? What is your favorite part of this passage? Mine is Zechariah 2:3-4. He's actually overhearing an angelic conversation! Did you know we could do that?

Chapter 2

My Divine Journey

by Joe Brock

This book is about the encounters Charity and I have with angels but I hope it can be more than that. Sharing our experiences is a good thing, but to write in such a way that awakens and inspires others to have their own experiences is a great thing. In my younger days as a believer, I would read amazing stories of people hearing God's voice, seeing visions, or having an encounter with an angel. These things mesmerized me. They also fostered a lie that I was not qualified to have these same experiences. I believed that the supernatural was reserved for the spiritually elite and I felt that just was not me.

So I lived in a dilemma: I had an insatiable desire to experience the supernatural, but a lie lodged in my heart that told me I couldn't have it. Through much prayer and pain, God started opening my eyes. Hope began to dawn in my heart and I began to accept and believe what the Bible said—that I was not just a physical being. The hunger for the supernatural came from a place inside of me that no one had told me existed. The life of the Spirit is for all people, because God designed all people to be spiritual.

It was never an esoteric designation—it was the fabric of our God-created composition.

As I embraced this and did a lot of repenting, I began to walk in the supernatural. I was blessed to be part of a group who were passionate to receive all God has for us and we grew together in our understanding and experience of supernatural Christianity. I began hearing God daily. I cast out demons, prophesied, engaged in spiritual warfare at home and abroad, and began interacting with and co-laboring with angels.

We followed no magic formula. Instead, we simply identified the lies we believed and replaced them with God's truth. There was a definite progression. God introduced new things, and as we became seasoned in one aspect of the supernatural, He would move us into a new arena to learn more. I am happy to say this has not stopped. The divine life was never about superstars with global ministries; it is about simple things like mothers prophesying destiny into their children's lives. It is about the factory worker binding the darkness over their workplace and releasing the Kingdom of Heaven into their day. The divine life was never given to just pastors, preachers, or prophets, but to policemen, politicians, and producers as well.

You and I are designed to live and flow in God's spiritual reality. It is my hope and desire to help the entire Church see this truth. As more of the Church knows her true identity, her capacity to fight victoriously will increase. We are part of the same family and team. It is in my best interest to help you see that you, at your very essence, are created to walk each day fully aware of the spiritual reality around you. So how do we do this? This is an excellent place to start.

Restoring My Sight

For days there had been a movie that kept popping up in my head. At this time in my walk with Jesus, my wife and I were learning to hear and recognize God's voice. It finally began to dawn on me that these reoccurring thoughts were from the Lord. I checked our local movie rental store, and fortunately, they had a copy. The title was "At First Sight," and Val Kilmer was the lead actor.

Kilmer portrays a blind masseuse who works at a ski lodge. A young woman comes to the lodge to get away from some personal issues. While there, the blind masseuse gives her a massage. They begin a relationship which leads the masseuse to undergo a medical procedure that restores his sight.

The movie depicts this blind man transitioning from interacting with the world primarily through sound to being able to see. This was the part of the movie God was highlighting for me. Up to this point, my primary way of living life was only through my natural senses. Just as this blind man was now able to see, God was giving me back my sight—my spiritual sight.

Two scenes really spoke to me about regaining sight. The first was when the doctor was slowly and carefully removing the gauze from the man's eyes after his surgery. As the dressing came off, his sight gradually returned and he saw a woman in his room. He fearfully called out to her, asking who she was and she responded, "I'm your sister."

At that moment something unforeseen happened. Until this time, the man's only real knowledge of his sister was through sound alone. When he finally *saw* her, he did not recognize her. His ability to see was now functional, but not yet instructed. It was when he took the knowledge of the reality he knew, hearing, and combined it with this new ability, sight, that the two realms merged into one. His new perception of what was real exploded into something miraculous. Over the years, he had only been able to interact with the world in a limited capacity. Now that his sight was restored, he was able to live and function at a higher level than ever before.

The second scene took place in front of his apartment. Each day he would stand in front of his home waiting for the public bus. His only perception of the bus was through the sound that it made. Now with his sight restored, his encounter with the bus took on a whole new meaning. Never once had he been able to see the size and power of a public bus. As he stood waiting, he recognized the sound of the bus but was extremely intimidated when he saw it. Trying to merge the sight of the bus with the sound of the bus was more than he could handle and resulted in a mental overload. This was the very same lesson I was learning.

Throughout my life, before I was saved, I was limited in my encounters with the world. After I was born of the Spirit, my spiritual eyesight was healed. I began encountering and interacting with the same world I always had, but now with opened eyes. It was exciting, and at times a bit overwhelming, but through much prayer and studying the Scriptures, God held my hand and made me feel secure. It took some time for me to get used to seeing things that I had been blinded to. I often felt the evil when a demonic spirit was present, but I had never been able to see it. As my spiritual eyes were healed, I began feeling *and* seeing.

As my spiritual eyesight was being restored, I received visions and saw things in the spiritual realm, but I never saw angels. For so long, all my prayer partners and I could see was the darkness: demons, deliverance, curses, wounds, and so on. I prayed to see the angelic realm but never really heard anything back from the Lord. Though I had seen angels as a child when they would come in my bedroom and talk to me, that was years ago.

Finally, after a long wait, the angels started becoming visible. In the last ten years I have begun to see the angelic again. In some seasons I see angels all the time, and at other times I have to focus my attention to see them. The angels are always there, but often my current circumstances can affect whether I recognize them.

Recently, the Lord told me why it took so long for me to see the angels. He said that there was little chance I would be lured into idolatry by seeing demons and the darkness. He explained that He waited until my love for Him went deep enough inside my heart that, as He began to show me the angelic and the things of His glory, I would not be lured away from Him by these. Demons are ugly, disgusting beings and I had no desire for them. By allowing my love for Jesus to deepen beyond the grandeur of angels, the Lord was protecting me. I pray it not take you as long to see angels, because as a Christian, all of this is available to you as well.

Our Creation

As a follower of Christ, for you to accept the fact that you can and should see the angelic, you need a stable biblical and theological foundation. This is imperative because when the enemy lies and says that this is not for you, you can stand on what God's Book says. So we will first look at the essence of our creation—both our being and the habitation God designed for us. Secondly, we will look at Jesus' conversation with Nicodemus in John 3. From these two places, you will see that you are created as a physical and spiritual being, and as a Christian, you were born again to walk in the unseen realms.

Genesis 1:26-27 tells us that God created us in His image. This is an amazing thought to consider. God used Himself as the standard when He designed us. We came into being when He blew His very life into the dust He had created. Our essence, therefore, is nothing less than the dust God created and God Himself!

Then the LORD God formed man of dust from the ground and breathed into his nostrils the breath of life, and man became a living being. (Genesis 2:7)

We are dirt and Spirit—or to put it into other terms, we are physical and spiritual. These are the two aspects of our design. God's voice spoke the world into existence and He formed us out of the earth's dust and then filled us with His breath. What came forth was a living being.

We are the dualistic result of both physical and spiritual elements. This is you, and this is me. We are not just flesh and blood, skin and bones, sinew and tissue. At our most basic design, we are the living, walking result of God's breath. In our very essence, we are part divine. We did not produce this divinity. No, we are the result of the pure brilliance of God's architecture.

In His wisdom, God did something else that completed this circle. Not only did He create us as physical and spiritual beings, but He also created a reality for us to live in that was designed to accommodate our essence. It would not make sense to give us such unbelievable capacity and then not give us a place to express it. He made it possible for us to live effortlessly in both the heavens and on the earth.

The Heavens and the Earth

In the beginning, God created the heavens and the earth. (Genesis 1:1)

Hopefully, you are beginning to recognize how multi-dimensional you are. You are the dust of this earth filled with the life of God Himself. This truth has the potential to awaken you to the vast and limitless potential you carry. We are all bound by the limitations of our creation, but it just so happens that we are created out of God's essence. I do not believe God intended us to live boring, uneventful lives. Since God gave us His life, His DNA, we should live lives that look like God. We live in a place where this is possible.

In Genesis 1:1 God created two things. First, He created the heavens. It is imperative you see that 'heavens' is not a singular noun; the word heavens is plural. Despite the fact that God created the universe with trillions of stars and planets, the only physical place He acknowledges explicitly is earth. The first words God wanted us to read in His eternal Word are what He created—the plural heavens and the singular earth. This speaks to a fundamental part of how God intends us to live; grasping the truths within these verses will enable you to see angels, have visions and dreams, and engage the very dwelling place of God.

Earth

All of us are familiar with earth. We know about dirt, trees, lakes, rivers, and oceans. We know about the climate and seasonal changes. We know about food, recreation, and family. All of these are physical, tangible things we see, hear, and encounter every day. We know when to put a sweater on or when to turn the air conditioner up. Our physical bodies live and exist in this material world, and although this is what God intended, we are more than physical beings. Just as our physical man knows how to live, act, and interact in the physical world, God created the heavens so our spiritual man can live and function as well.

The Heavens

The Bible speaks of three heavens. By knowing what the three heavens are and how they relate to us, we can expand the way we live in unimaginable ways.

The First Heaven

The Bible explicitly describes the heavenly sky comprised of the physical atmosphere above us and the sun, moon, and stars.

When I consider Thy heavens, the work of Thy fingers, The moon and the stars, which Thou hast ordained. (Psalm 8:3)

Lift up your eyes and look to the heavens: Who created all these? He who brings out the starry host one by one and calls forth each of them by name. (Isaiah 40:26 NIV)

The second heaven is a little more difficult to explain so we will discuss the third heaven next and then come back to the second heaven.

The Third Heaven

Paul describes the third Heaven in his second letter to the Corinthians:

I know a man in Christ who fourteen years ago—whether in the body I do not know, or out of the body I do not know, God knows—such a man was caught up to the third heaven. ...was caught up into Paradise, and heard inexpressible words, which a man is not permitted to speak (2 Cor. 12:2, 4).

In these passages, Paul describes the third Heaven as Paradise. From what we can gather scripturally, this is a place of overwhelming amazement and beauty. I believe this is God's personal dwelling place and abode. This is also the place where Jesus told the man on the cross next to Him they would meet that very day. Theologians believe Paul is describing an experience he personally had where he went to this heavenly place while still physically alive. Whether he went there in his physical body or his spirit went, Paul had a personal experience with and in the third Heaven.

The Second Heaven

The Bible does not specifically tell us what and where the second heaven is, but we do know of the natural heavenly sky and Paul speaks of a third Heaven, so it is logical to conclude there is a second heaven. My personal belief (based on both my experience and my reading of the Bible) is that a spiritual reality or realm that was negatively affected by the fall of man wraps around the earth. This is where the powers and principalities that Paul speaks of in Ephesians 6 exist and they contend for the hearts of men. This second heaven is the realm of spiritual warfare, where the god of this age wages war against Christ and His church.

> *To me, the very least of all saints, this grace was given, to preach to the Gentiles the unfathomable riches of Christ, and to bring to light what is the administration of the mystery which for ages has been hidden in God who created all things; so that the manifold wisdom of God might now be made known through the church to the rulers and the authorities in the heavenly places.* (Ephesians 3:8-10)

In Daniel 10, the Prince of Persia holds up an angel who was sent in response to Daniel's prayer. In Luke 10:18, Luke writes that Jesus saw satan fall out of heaven like lightening. I believe that both these events occurred in the second heaven. Many of my encounters with the demonic and the angelic realms have occurred in the second heaven. Let me share one with you.

A month or so ago we purchased a new-to-us vehicle. We had been praying and God gave us better than we were asking for. My wife drove me to pick it up, dropped me off, and then headed home. I followed shortly behind. As I was pulling out onto the highway to go home, I saw an angel sitting on the hood of the vehicle with his arms crossed over his chest. His right leg was crossed over his left with his left leg apparently resting on the bumper. He never looked at me or acknowledged me; he just sat there looking ahead. I asked the Lord who he was and why he was there. The Lord told me he was my assistant and that he was there to assist me in the things pertaining to our lives. I was immediately filled with joy knowing that no aspect of my life was without God's care and protection. I love when these things happen!

John Wimber said we are living between D-day and V-day. We are in that time period between the beginning of the war and final consummation of all things in Christ. The enemy would love to sell me a lemon or have someone take advantage of me. By inviting Jesus and the angels into our daily lives, we are poised for daily miracles. This may be foreign and new to some of you, but the Bible allows for such things. I pray as you become open, you will have stories like this too.

How Do You See, Joe?

I have been asked how I am able to see things like this. The answer really is quite simple... because they are there and I have been born again to see them. I have a spirit that was brought back to life at my conversion. Now that I am spiritually alive, I can see, hear, feel, touch, and flow in the spiritual realm. I have seen numerous angels, had countless dreams and visions, and have taken multiple trips into both the heavenly places and into parts of Heaven itself.

Here is the thing though: I am no different than you if you are born again. Living in the spiritual realm is not about having a special gift, calling, or anointing just as we do not need a special gift or anointing to be able to sense the physical world. All we have to do is be born into it. My longing is for you to see that you were created by God to live in the heavenly places, too.

Born from Above

As discussed, our human design is both physical and spiritual. When Adam and Eve fell, their spirit broke their connection with God and, just as God said would happen, they spiritually died. At that point, God put a plan into action that was fulfilled 4000 years later when a Jewish carpenter named Jesus died on God's sacrificial altar. This death and subsequent resurrection opened a door of opportunity to anyone who would accept this Jesus and put their trust in Him. The answer is to be born again.

In John 3, Jesus speaks with a Pharisee named Nicodemus. Many of the Pharisees hated Jesus, but Nicodemus was different. He saw something in Jesus that intrigued him and he visited Jesus under the cover of darkness. Nicodemus confessed that he saw a supernatural aspect to Jesus and concluded that His miracles were possible because God was with Him.

Jesus' response goes right to the heart of the matter: to be able to perceive God's Kingdom, you must be born again, from above (see John 3:3 ISV). Jesus told Nicodemus that the miracles were a byproduct of living under God's divine reign and rule. For Nicodemus to perceive and experience this in his own life, he must experience a second, spiritual birth. Nicodemus was confused, so Jesus explained what being born again means.

> *Jesus answered, "Truly, truly, I say to you, unless one is born of water and the Spirit, he cannot enter into the kingdom of God. That which is born of the flesh is flesh, and that which is born of the Spirit is spirit. Do not marvel that I said to you, 'You must be born again [from above].' The wind blows where it wishes and you hear the sound of it, but do not know where it comes from and where it*

is going; so is everyone who is born of the Spirit." (John 3:5-8 ESV)

The phrase "born again" can be confusing. How can we, being already alive, experience a second birth? Looking at this phrase in the original Greek, however, sheds light on the concept and offers profound insights.

The word "born" in this passage is the Greek word *gennao* (pronounced gen-na-o). It carries the primary meaning of being fathered or sired. The word translated "again" in most English versions is the Greek adverb *anothen* (pronounced an-o-th-en) and literally means "from above."

In this verse, the word "from above" modifies the word "born." Jesus told Nicodemus that being born again means you must receive a second fathering or siring. Our first birth speaks of our natural birth and our natural father, while our second, spiritual birth speaks of being born from above and our heavenly Father.

We were born of the earth and we were reborn of Heaven at the moment of our salvation. This gives us dual-citizenship. I am a member of the human community, and I am now a member of the heavenly community. Because I was born of the Spirit, that realm and reality are now just as much my home as the earth has been. Therefore, seeing into the heavens should become just as normal as seeing on the earth because they are now both my home. That is why we pray that the eyes of our hearts would be enlightened—so we can see our spiritual home more clearly (see Eph. 1:18).

Once you are born again, your spiritual faculties are alive. Your flesh is of the physical, but your spirit is now of the heavenlies.

I encourage you to pray into this revelation of your identity as a supernatural child of God and what that means in your everyday life.

Ask the Holy Spirit to teach you about your born again, spiritual nature as you meditate on these truths from His Word and ask Him what it means to have His angels render service to you.

1. You Are Both Physical and Spiritual

    Then the Lord God formed man of dust from the ground, and breathed into his nostrils the breath of life; and man became a living being. (Genesis 2:7)

2. You Were Born Again (from Above)

    Jesus answered, "Truly, I tell you emphatically, unless a person is born of water and Spirit he cannot enter the kingdom of God. What is born of the flesh is flesh, and what is born of the Spirit is spirit. Don't be astonished that I told you, 'All of you must be born from above.' The wind blows where it wants to. You hear its sound, but you don't know where it comes from or where it is going. That's the way it is with everyone who is born of the Spirit." (John 3:5-8 ISV)

3. If You Are Saved and a Follower of Jesus, YOU Have Everyday Angels

    Are they not all ministering spirits, sent out to render service for the sake of those who will inherit salvation? (Hebrews 1:14)

As I bring this chapter to a close, I want to reiterate that you were created, designed, and reborn to live in this spiritual reality. Heaven IS your home now, not just when you pass away. Regain your fullness as a human with all the awe and wonder God built into you. Enjoy the trees, the mountains, and the rivers, but now enjoy the visions, dreams, and the amazing angels all around you, too.

What About You?

- What has your life with Christ been like? If angels have not been a part of your spiritual journey, then all you need to do is ask the Lord to help make them real to you. According to Matthew 7:7-8, you WILL see angelic involvement in your life if you ask, seek, and knock. Have you asked? What was the result?

- Until now, have you ever considered the magnitude of your design? If so, what have your conclusions been? If you have not, can you now begin to see what God intends for His children? How does this make you feel?

- Are you familiar with the phrase "born again"? Have you been born from above? If you are not completely sure of your salvation, you can be. Please refer to Appendix A of this book *How to Be Born of the Spirit* and find out more at www.BornOfTheSpirit.Today.

- After reading this chapter, how do you feel about being fathered by a heavenly Father? Consider the fact that you now have dual-citizenship. What does that mean to you?

Chapter 3

Look-Alike Angels: Their Personas, Personalities and Preferences

by Charity Kayembe

I told my hairdresser that I would like some soft highlights for the summer. I had gone with a darker color for a while, but now I wanted to change it up a bit with more of a sun-kissed look. I told her, "Just go a little bit lighter."

Famous last words. Even she was surprised at the color and used the term "platinum" to describe the new bleached version of my hair. The next day, a colleague walked into my office and called me "blondie." *Awesome.*

Now, I really didn't mind because it had actually turned out quite nice, but it was definitely unexpected. So imagine my surprise when my angel Shobi got incredibly excited about my new look and told me how perfect it was.

"We match! Now you're my mini-me! You look like my kid sister. Don't you see the resemblance? This is great!"

(Note: Shobis is the more traditional golden hair, eyes of fire, luminous kind of angel. Pojes is tall, dark, and handsome. They are like an older and younger brother to me; totally a sibling vibe between us.)

I figured Shobi was just doing his job of protecting my peace and not wanting me to get upset. I smiled and nodded and didn't think much of it. What are you supposed to do with comments like that? I had no grid for this.

Peter's Angel

Well, wouldn't you know, just a couple days later I was on a plane and had "happened" to grab a copy of *Charisma* magazine to read on the flight. Inside, it just "happened" to have an article on angels. The late prophetic leader John Paul Jackson wrote about the angel who helped Peter escape from prison. When Peter knocked on the gate of Mary's house, the other disciples didn't even let him in because they thought it wasn't actually Peter. They assumed it was just his angel (see Acts 12:5-16).

John Paul said that many biblical scholars understand these verses to indicate that our guardian angels can sound and even look like us. Really?

"Shobi, it turns out you might actually be right about this!" (I know, oh me of little faith.)

He just smiled, tipped his head to the side and shrugged, "Told you..."

Lord of Angel Armies

While we are discussing the appearance of angels, it may also be a good time to mention their wings, or lack thereof. This was the topic of another conversation I had with my heavenly friends one morning. Obviously, my angels can appear to me however they want. Sometimes we see angels in their full knock-me-on-the-ground glory and other times it is so subtle we don't even realize they are not human beings (see Heb. 13:2). Usually my guys go with the latter, and I don't see feathers because of this.

Even though this does not matter to me at all, I did try teasing them about it just for fun. "Oh man. Of all the angels in all of Heaven, I get assigned the wingless ones? What did you guys do, miss the line when they were handing them out?"

They just smiled knowingly at each other, as if they were trying to decide if they should let me in on their secret.

Now around this same time, I had also been giving them a bit of a hard time about the execution of their guardianship responsibilities. I would say things like, "Guys, are you even actually protecting me? Are you even paying attention? You're having way too much fun. Shouldn't you be carefully watching out for my physical safety and wellbeing here?"

The impression I got back from them was, "We have people for that." (With the idea of "people" being some other, presumably more responsible, angels.)

My Security Detail

After all of that, they decided to enlighten me, and it was almost like they flipped a switch and turned on the houselights. It was as if we had been under a spotlight, but now it was bright all around us. I was able to see a lot further out into the spirit realm, and I realized that we were literally surrounded (not unlike 2 Kings 6:17).

Angels—of the winged variety, I might add—were standing at the ready. They were definitely paying attention! I could see rows upon rows of them in every direction.

"See guys, now that is what I'm talking about. That instills confidence!"

Of course, I knew that there are many more angels around than I see every day. I love that they are called an "innumerable company" (see Heb. 12:22 KJV). When the Bible uses terms like "myriads of myriads," you definitely get the feeling there are more than enough angels to go around (see Rev. 5:11). They are not being rationed out, so I don't need to be afraid they might not be around when I need them.

This is God's Army. And they are protecting God's kids! They see that as the honor of a lifetime, and they are not about to mess it up, which means I can rest assured knowing these guys, who are bigger and faster and stronger than I am, are on the case. And that frees me up to not worry ... about anything, really.

While it seemed like Pojes and Shobis had been holding out on me, since it took them so long to finally introduce me to their friends, I didn't mind. I just realized, yet again, that they were absolutely right about everything they had said.

Turns out they really do have people for that.

But Seriously... What's Up with the Wings?

It is very interesting to note that in the hundreds of Scriptures recording angelic encounters, most of them do not make any mention of wings. Of course, we don't make an argument from scriptural silence, and just because they are not mentioned does not mean none of those angels had wings. However, many of the verses about angels do make it clear they were wingless.

In the story of God saving Lot and his family in Genesis 19, the original Hebrew actually goes back and forth between calling the two messengers from God "angels" in verse one and "men" in verse ten, then "angels" in verse fifteen and "men" in verse sixteen. And instead of mentioning wings or feathers, Scripture records their hands and what they did with them (see Gen. 19:10).

Daniel had extended back and forth conversations with angels, and he consistently referred to them as men:

- Gabriel stood before him as "one who looked like a man" (Dan. 8:15-16).

- "The man Gabriel" came in the vision and gave him instructions (Dan. 9:21-22).

- He looked and behold there was "a certain man" dressed in linen (Dan. 10:5).

- "One who resembled a human being" was with him and he spoke to him (Dan. 10:16).

- Then the "one with human appearance" touched him and strengthened him (Dan. 10:18).

Similarly, in the New Testament we see angels being referred to as "men" and people "dressed in white" (see Luke 24:4; Acts 1:10). And obviously the very fact that we can entertain angels without realizing it confirms that oftentimes they will look like people (see Heb. 13:2).

Recording artist and healing revivalist Joshua Mills knows his three angels by name and testifies they look very similar to him in appearance—just bigger and with more muscles! My favorite part of Joshua's testimony is that he was introduced to his angels in a dream. That dream encounter marked the beginning of a re-awakening of the angelic realm in his life and now he regularly sees and partners with them in ministry, even conducting Angel Schools to activate others into this realm. Indeed, dreams are bridges to the supernatural!

Over and over the Bible refers to angels appearing just like us. This is huge! One reason why more believers haven't seen their angels is because they haven't understood what they are looking for. Once we know what we're looking for, it is easier to see.

What an Angel Wants

We know that angels have free will, because satan is an angel and chose to disobey God. Scripture also makes it clear that angels have feelings, and my angels are no exception (see 1 Pet. 1:12 and Job 38:7). Upon realizing this, I wanted to know if there was anything I could do for them, since they both take such good care of me. I wondered if I could ever return the favor in some small way, so I asked them how I might be able to thank them for their great service.

Shobis said, "A simple 'good morning' will do it for me, Milady. I can go all day on a good morning from you!"

I learned then that it was really just the idea of acknowledgement. I could honor him by addressing and greeting him instead of ignoring him. That certainly didn't seem like too much to ask. Until I checked with Poje, and his request was even simpler than that.

"Just a look, Milady. A quick moment to catch your eye. I don't need you to *say* anything." (He said this as he coughed "ahem," while throwing Shobi a teasing grin.) "But actually, I would welcome your looks several times a day. I mean, whenever you might think of it and get the chance...."

"Wow, guys," I responded. "These requests almost seem like they are more for me than for you! This is totally going to help me. Just not sure how exactly they are such a blessing for you—especially you, Poje? I mean, just looking over at you for a moment? Not even saying anything to you, or listening to anything you have to say? Just a look, really?"

Watch the Watchers

"It is actually quite simple, Milady," Pojes went on to explain. "The truth is you are always safe and protected. Whether you see us here watching out for you or not, whether you feel safe and protected or not—you ARE. And as long as you are safe and sound, then I am doing my job, and Father and Jesus are pleased with My service to them in guarding you.

"The thing is, though, I would love to go above and beyond my call of duty in serving God, if at all possible. I mean, Jesus is just so in love with you, and He cares so much about your happiness and your peace. It brings Him tremendous pleasure when you are in a good place emotionally. He is pleased when you feel safe, protected, and secure. He cares more about your inner equilibrium and state of being than even you do sometimes. He just cares!

"Anyway, I know that if I can get you to look at me, just to lock eyes with me for even a moment in the middle of your full and busy day, then you will know greater peace. You will feel more confident and safe because you will see and feel and know and understand deep down that you are not alone. You are being watched over. You are being cared for. We are all in this together with you and you face nothing by yourself. We are a team and a family in the sense that we are all created by Father and live to serve Him forever.

"And I want you to feel that togetherness, that not aloneness. I want you to feel that comfort and joy that come from knowing you are seen. You have a witness to your life. We are right here with you and see everything you do and say, and nothing goes unnoticed. You are appreciated and admired. You are loved.

"We do love you, Milady. How could we not? It's clear to see why Jesus is so totally taken by you—you are a woman after His own heart. You care about the things He cares about. You do things with Him that He likes to do. Your heart is always for Him. You are always concerned about what pleases Him and would make Him happy. You have made Him your whole world! How easy, then, is it for us to equally reciprocate those feelings back to you."

Accepted by Angels

Author and artist Dr. Marie Chapian also describes how loved and accepted angels make her feel. She has been good friends with her personal angels for many years and in her book *Angels in Our Lives*, she writes:

> When I'm hard at work in my writing studio I sense the presence of angels. An angel might stand behind me; he is enormous, taller than my ceiling, and his presence fills the room. Always when the angels appear, I feel a sense of confidence and peace. Immediately the tension I may not have been aware of in my shoulders and neck relaxes and I feel washed over with the complete acceptance and a renewed sense of well-being.
>
> I breathe in the beauty of the moment and stop working to praise and thank the Lord, and when I resume my place at my desk, it feels as if I had spent hours lying on the beach listening to the surf. I feel loved and beautiful, and best of all, I feel accepted.
>
> Something the Lord is teaching me and I am learning from being in the presence of angels – and not just when I'm in the presence of one angel, but when huge crowds of angels appear before me – I feel accepted. Not a single hair

of fault-finding or distrust, competition, or intimidation wafts into the air. It's an unfamiliar sensation, this one of total acceptance, and I want to hold onto, become familiar with, live in, and project to others.

The angels' personalities are accepting. To feel so much pure, divine acceptance is like taking a bath in a sunrise.[4]

Angelic experiences like these both encourage us and make us fall even more in love with Jesus, because He fashioned angels! What a brilliantly creative way to help and bless us. See how great a love He has lavished upon us? God's compassion for us knows no bounds and is expressed through the gift of His ministering spirits, the angels, whom He sent to render service for His beloved children (see Heb. 1:14).

Angel Diaries: Daniel 10

Things really came together for me one night after work. My husband Leo had a meeting that evening so I was happy to have an extended quiet time when I got home. Shobi wanted to show me something in Daniel, so I turned there and started reading and listening to him share his perspective on the verses.

Shobi was saying something… And then, all of a sudden, I woke up. What? When did I fall asleep? I glanced at my phone—7:33. Oh my word, it's almost 8am! I need to get ready for work!

I noticed the bedroom door. It was open, which was strange. I shut it quietly when I get up early and… where's Leo? He wouldn't have gotten up just to open the door. I looked out the window—he wasn't swimming his laps. I didn't hear the free weights clanking around in the basement either.

Leo was not in the bedroom, he wasn't downstairs or outside. What in the world? Where was he? Wait, what day is it again? Ohhhh. It's

7:33 at night. Right. So, I just happened to fall deeply asleep, in a sitting position, in broad daylight, and be so out of it I had no idea what was going on?

Breaking It Down

Shobi interjected, "Welcome to Daniel chapter 10, verse 5, through and especially, verse 9. Daniel had a vision of an angel, heard the sounds of the angel's words. And as soon as he heard them, Daniel fell into a deep sleep."

I said, "Really? You had to literally knock me out for this?"

Apparently, Shobi wanted to get my attention and help me realize this section of Scripture was a special word for me in that moment. I'm living it, so don't miss it! He highlighted some of verses 18, 19 and 20 as well....

> *Then this one with human appearance touched me again and strengthened me. He said, "O man of high esteem, do not be afraid. Peace be with you; take courage and be courageous!" Now as soon as he spoke to me, I received strength and said, "May my lord speak, for you have strengthened me." Then he said, "Do you understand why I came to you?"* (Daniel 10:18-20)

Shobi explained, "See, all of this is what we do for you. You want a biblical example of it—this is it. We strengthen you. We are all about keeping the peace, right? Encouraging you with joy, and letting you not be afraid. Not to mention how helpful I am at breaking it all down for you and giving you understanding about things (wink). It is all right there. AND even our name for you can be found here if you have eyes to see it."

"Milady"

(Note: Quite often my angels will address me as "Milady." A term of respect and also endearment, and I think more than anything the reason they use it is because just hearing that one word makes me smile. It is such a fun little title! So that is what he is commenting about.)

He continued, "Daniel was called a 'man of high esteem,' and you have a note in your Bible that says it could also be translated man of 'desirability' or 'preciousness.' See? It is the same exact thing. There's respect, there's affirmation, there's honor and affection. It's essentially 'Milady'—just a guy version of it. Anyway, all of this isn't even the best part. Keep reading...."

In the first year of Darius the Mede, I arose to be an encouragement and a protection for him. (Daniel 11:1)

"Did you see it?" Shobi asked. "We angels gave courage to Daniel (see Dan. 10:19), and he turned around and gave it to those he was called to minister to. That's what I'm talking about! Not only that, check out the literal Hebrew translation of the word 'encouragement.' It means 'strengthener.'

"What we did for Daniel empowered him to do the same for others. And you know that he wasn't a warrior for Darius, not a valiant soldier giving him strength and protection. He did it with words! Daniel gave Darius God's perspective on things, and that encouraged him— just like we do with you. We help make sure you are seeing life from a divine, heavenly point of view, and that protects your joy and peace and encourages your heart.

"And when you are in a joyful, peaceful, courageous place, you are much more ready to be a blessing and encouragement to those around you, right? If you are anxious or stressed or angry or afraid, you are sure not looking for opportunities to minister life to others. You're just trying to keep your act together and avoid falling apart!

"Enter our awesome helpfulness, which places you in a much better position, ready for ministry, ready to be a blessing and give courage, and ready to help strengthen everyone around you. That is the vision, Milady. That is what we are going for. And don't you see how God gets much more glory from your peace and joy than your stress and fear? Of course He does."

Shobi was right. Now I can do for others what God and His angels have done for me. I can comfort others with the comfort I have received (see 2 Cor. 1:4). I become more aware of the feelings of others, as I see just how aware God is of mine, and how aware my angels are of mine. They are giving their whole lives, during my whole life, to make sure I feel well, peaceful, joyful, and loved.

Dream Come True

Romans 14:17 tells us that righteousness, peace, and joy are the very Kingdom of God. Peace and joy? They are just emotions, for goodness' sake. Could they really be that important? Jesus showed me how He feels about emotions and confirmed my angelic revelation through a dream.

In the book *Hearing God Through Your Dreams*,[5] my father Mark and I teach there are heavenly messages even in our weird and crazy dreams. By simply decoding the pictures, we can understand the meaning in them. This dream is a great example of that. There were a few different symbols that illustrated Matthew 11:25-30 ("Come to Me, all who are weary and heavy-laden, and I will give you rest..."), but the part I want to explain is about yolks.

In the dream I was trying to make eggs, but all the yolks were little stones—they were as hard as rocks! That didn't seem quite right, and it wasn't working at all. Well, what is the opposite of a hard yolk? That would be an easy yoke—which, incidentally, is the kind Jesus wants me to have.

I journaled Jesus' interpretation of the dream:

> "Hey, I know you're exhausted from all you're doing, so come and relax. You are trying to make it work, but you are making it too hard. I have a gentle and humble heart, so learn from Me. I'll make your work easy and help you find rest for your soul."

Rest for what? Not my body. My soul. My emotional equilibrium and inner state of being are what those in the heavenly dimension are most concerned with. First and foremost, they want us to have rest and peace inside. Jesus says He personally is in a healthy place—gentle and humble in heart—and He invites us to join Him there. He showed me, through dreaming about Scripture, "This is it. This is what I'm talking about. This is for you, for now: a rested soul, an easy yoke, a peaceful heart."

These stories and Scriptures have highlighted how God and His company of Heaven care about us, our hearts, and our everyday lives. In the next chapter, we will get a glimpse of the other end of the spectrum, where God's angel armies are involved in protecting one of the most influential cities in the world, and how we can partner with them in strategic, supernatural Kingdom alliance.

What About You?

- Read Acts 12:15, Matthew 18:10, Psalm 34:7, and Psalm 91:11-12. Billy Graham taught that these verses affirm we all have guardian angels assigned to us. What do these verses mean to you?

- Read Daniel 8:15-16 and 9:20-23. Did God want Daniel to listen to the angel? Was the angel a reliable messenger?

- Would you be open to receiving a word from God through an angel?

- Have you ever experienced that?

Chapter 4

Barriers of Angels in the Boroughs of New York City

by Joe Brock

In the mid-1990's I was associated with a group that was actively involved in inner healing and deliverance ministries. As their ministry evolved, God began sending various members of our team on short-term mission trips to confront and pull down powers and principalities in strategic areas throughout the world. In 1996, I made my first trip out of the United States to do prayer warfare in the Philippines. It was a life-changing experience, and little did I know, these journeys would become a regular part of my life.

Beginning on My Own

The first few trips I went on were always with other people, and over time my role changed and developed. By the early 2000s my time with this ministry had come to an end, and with this, I believed these trips had also concluded. I incorrectly assumed that my involvement in this type of prayer ministry was only because I was a part of this group. In time, God moved on me in a personal way and showed me that such prayer journeys would be part of my on-going ministry.

When God began to send me on my own, my calling and gifts began to grow and emerge. I learned a good lesson through this. It is often necessary to follow others for a season, but there may come a time when we bless and honor our leaders and move on to walk in our unique and personal calling.

Much of what I do now has very little resemblance to what I did with this group. They gave me a great foundation. From this foundation God was able to show me how He wanted me to minister.

> *Now there are **varieties** of gifts, but the same Spirit. And there are **varieties** of ministries, and the same Lord. There are **varieties** of effects, but the same God who works all things in all persons.* (1 Corinthians 12:4-6)

We are not supposed to duplicate others' callings or ways of ministering; we are to let Jesus expand His life and purposes inside of us so that we develop into the people He has called us to be. God is diverse enough to make each person, ministry, and church look very little like anyone or anything else. It is only as we let go and explore the wisdom and desires of the Spirit that we emerge as the creations God has designed us to be.

These ministry trips each have a specific purpose. Some have been about confronting cultural idols and breaking their power off the minds of the local people. Others have been going into geographic areas of intense darkness and releasing the Glory of the Lord to alleviate spiritual blindness in the region. For a long time, the majority of the trips dealt with the darkness and the demonic. Over the last couple of years, things have begun to change. The stories I am going to share are not going to be in the chronological order they occurred, but rather in the order I understand the Lord wants them written. My first story is actually one of the more recent trips. It begins with something God spoke to me close to a year ago.

A Growing Collaboration with the Angelic

As my dealings with the angelic began to increase, God came to me one day and said something that took some time to accept and be at peace with. While in prayer, the Lord said to me, "Joe, I am releasing to you a brigade of angels to be in your charge." Of course, when you hear something like this, it catches you off guard. What did this mean? What am I supposed to do with them? How many are in a brigade? I prayed and sought the Lord and the answers began to come.

The Lord showed me that there has been a coalition between the angelic realm and the human race since creation. Humans were endowed to be the caretakers of this world under the jurisdiction of God's authority. In the Fall of Man, we surrendered our rights to satan, but through the Cross, Jesus took these rights back and called us to go into all the world under His authority to fulfill our created mandate.

It is now within the context of our calling that mankind and the angelic are to co-labor to bring about God's desires on earth. God told me that He would teach me how to properly work with the angels with whom I have been entrusted. The next few trips would help train me on how to partner effectively with them. This became the basis for my most recent journey to New York City.

Heading to New York City

Just before the 2016 presidential election, the Lord told me to go to New York City with my son. We were to travel within the five boroughs of New York City to establish a barrier of angels for the purpose of "draining the evil out." This phrase—"drain the evil out"—was the exact phrase I heard God speak to me.

Over the next few days, the Lord outlined four specific geographic places I would travel to. At each of these spots, I would release 500 angels. The four locations were the furthest points north, south, east, and west of the five boroughs of New York City. After examining them on a map, I realized they formed a diamond shape. Once the angels were released, they would create a spiritual barrier with a twofold purpose. First, it is to hold the demonic and darkness from being able to enter this area. Second, it is to act as a filter allowing the existing evil to drain out.

In late October of 2016, my son and I began our journey to New York. Our first stop was in Washington D.C. where the Lord had us pray at a couple of different locations. Immediately after this, we made the drive north to New York and began navigating to each of our four spots.

I don't know if you have ever tried to drive throughout New York City, but if you have, you can appreciate what that day looked and felt like. Fast driving, lots of traffic, and expensive tolls everywhere you went. Over the course of the day, we successfully made it to each of our assigned destinations. By day's end, there were now 2000 angels creating a diamond-shaped wall or barrier within the four boroughs of New York City.

This day was unique for me. On these trips I take, I have come to expect God to show me what is happening in the spirit realm. On this particular journey, however, I was not given any spiritual insight at all. Not once did I see an angel either with us or released as we prayed. There were no visions or revelations of what transpired because of our prayers. Looking back, this was to build our trust in Him. God gives us what we need, not always what we want. On this part of the trip, this was the case. We just had to choose to trust and believe that God was still fully overseeing our entire mission.

What Do You Think?

As I have shared this story, I have received mixed responses. Some people seem amazed; others doubt that things like this are real. I truly want this book to inspire you to consider how the Lord wants you to be interacting with the angelic. If you do not agree or have doubts about what you read, please go back to the Scriptures and with an open heart, read passages about angels and let God minister to you. The last verse of the Apostle John's gospel says:

> *And there are also many other things which Jesus did, which if they were written in detail, I suppose that even the world itself would not contain the books that would be written.* (John 21:25)

I see a couple things here. First, what we saw Jesus do in the Bible was just a glimpse into what His short, three-year ministry truly looked like. Second, the fact that God included this verse in the Bible tells me that we are to not limit ourselves to *only* what the Bible says. Now let me be clear here, the Bible establishes what Jesus' ministry looked like. But Jesus Himself said we would do greater things:

> *Truly, truly, I say to you, he who believes in Me, the works that I do shall he do also; and greater works than these shall he do; because I go to the Father* (John 14:12).

The word 'greater' here comes from the Greek word μέγας (*megas*) where we get the English word mega. In its fuller definition, it carries the idea of 'greater' both quantitatively and qualitatively. This is exciting to consider. Jesus said that the people who place their trust in Him will have the capacity to do more of the miraculous than Jesus in sheer volume, and the miracles they will perform can actually surpass what Jesus did in size and splendor. Please do not exclude the angelic from this. My story is one of the thousands that are out there now.

Angels are looking for their human counterparts to learn from the Lord and begin to work with them to do what God is asking in this time of history. When you take what John said of "the many other things Jesus did," and couple this with the quantity and quality possibilities of what we can do, we should be astounded at what we see and be prepared for what is next. God could astonish us much more often than we currently allow.

> *But to which of the angels has He ever said, "Sit at My right hand, until I make your enemies a footstool for your feet"? Are they not all ministering spirits, sent out to render service for the sake of those who will inherit salvation?* (Hebrews 1:13-14)

God makes it clear that angels are dispatched to serve those who will inherit salvation. If you are a believer, that is you. As the redeemed, we inherit salvation and part of the lifestyle of the redeemed is the involvement of the angelic realm. What does this look like? The answer is we truly do not fully know. What is happening on the other side of the veil is beyond words, but it is exciting to see the curtain is getting thinner and thinner.

Our encounters with angels should happen as often as we need to be served. God has already sent some to you and for you. I just hope and pray you allow your eyes to see them. Look again at the Bible and see all the interaction mankind had with the angels. Are the humans in the Bible any more loved or precious to God than you? The answer is no. You have every right to grow into the knowledge and revelation of the angelic realm.

Drain the Evil

The trip to New York was different than any previous mission. This is not uncommon. Each time God sends me somewhere, something always seems to pop up that I have never seen or encountered before. This was no exception. On this trip, I never once saw an angel. On every other trip, I saw angels and interacted with them. On this one to New York City, I saw nothing. I believe God does this to keep us dependent on Him. Even though I did not see any angels, God was faithful to confirm the success of our trip.

I shared earlier that at the beginning of the commission for this trip, God clearly said on more than one occasion He wanted us to drain the evil. The word "drain" was highlighted and the mental imagery God gave was an angelic boundary with evil on the inside of the boundary slowly draining out.

This trip took place within a couple weeks of the presidential election. Once we returned and got somewhat settled, I received a phone call very early one morning from a family member who had received an encouraging prophetic dream about our mission prior to our departure. She asked if I had been paying attention to the news. Because I had been traveling, I had not. In excitement, she said that the most popular hash tagged phrase for the last two weeks had been #draintheswamp.

Donald Trump used this very phrase while he campaigned. I am aware this phrase was used in previous political venues, but since Trump is from New York City and we had just returned from a prayer trip to drain the evil from the city, I was convinced this was God's way of telling us we accomplished our mission.

I never imagined I would be involved in the things I am. I never dreamed I would travel the world, let alone do so partnering with angels. I am learning that my grid of God cannot become so rigid that I oppose something new He is trying to teach. God's Book is a truly safe place to look to when we need answers that transcend our current paradigm. If it is in the Bible or aligns with biblical truth, it is safe for you and me. I have a Father who promised if I ask for good, I will *only* get that which is good. It is exciting to know that it is God who wants us to work alongside our everyday angels.

Do Your Own Research

I encourage you to do your own study of angels. If you do not have your own Bible software, there are a number of free online resources available for you, such as e-Sword.

To get you started, we have included an appendix that lists all of the verses in the Bible about angels. We encourage you to meditate on these Scriptures and ask Holy Spirit to teach you through His Word. As you do this, you will gain a strong biblical framework for angelic interaction and a hunger for supernatural encounters will grow in you. This will build your faith, which will in turn activate a sensitivity and awareness for the company of Heaven, allowing you to personally experience what you have been reading about. The Bible is meant to be lived!

What About You?

Have you ever researched the topic of angels in Scripture before? What were some of your discoveries? References on angels are available in Appendix C for you to prayerfully meditate on.

- Has God ever given you an assignment? If so, do you feel it was successful? Why or why not?

- In your everyday life and the assignments God has for you, do you believe partnering with angels would be beneficial? In what ways? What do you envision might be accomplished for the Kingdom with such a coalition?

Chapter 5

Personal Angels: Our Match Made in Heaven

by Charity Kayembe

We know that angels are here to help us, so what are some of the ways my angels assist me and how is it different from the Lord's personal intervention? After all, I am a daughter of God! What do they know that I don't, and how did they find it out anyway?

One reason angels know more than we do is because they have been around a lot longer. They have seen more, so they understand how things work. For example, they are obviously familiar with the enemy's tactics. They also know more about Heaven and our heavenly Father. They have been watching and learning from Father, Jesus, and Holy Spirit for (almost) forever. I just showed up a few decades ago; my angels have been serving Father for millennia. They know what blesses Him more than I do. They know what Jesus likes better than I do.

In a Multitude of Counselors

When Esther prepared to spend her night with the king, she talked with Hegai, the king's eunuch. All the maidens could pick anything they wanted for the evening, but Esther recognized that Hegai knew the king much better than she did, so she asked for his recommendation. She followed his advice, and as a result, she found favor (see Esther 2:15).

Similarly, we are betrothed to Christ and want to bless, love, and serve Jesus and Father in ways they appreciate most. What's best for them? How do they like to be worshiped? What do they enjoy hearing whispered from the lips of their children? What makes them laugh and brings them the most pleasure?

Since angels have been observing various acts of service and worship expressed from millions of God's children down through the ages, they have more insight than we do. So in a way, angels can be our own personal Hegais, advising us on how best to serve our King. They know more than we do simply because they have been around longer, spent more time with Him than we have, and have seen His relationships play out over and over again.

I threw my husband Leo a surprise party shortly after we were married, and I wanted it to be extra special. So unbeknownst to him, I talked with his family, who had known him all his life. That way I could get everything just perfect and exactly how he would want it to be.

And so it is with Jesus.

We want to love Him in *His* love language. And while the irony of trying to "surprise" an omniscient God is not lost on me, I still think He appreciates the gesture. He says we captivate His heart with a single glance of our eyes (see Song of Sol. 4:9). When He feels that much for us, how can we not give Him our best love in return?

This is one way that interacting with angels is still ultimately about Jesus. We do not interact with angels for their sake. They would never stand for that! They always defer to God. Always talk about Jesus. Always and only have His interests and work at heart. The reason that I am my angels' whole world is because I am their assignment. They bless Father by taking care of me because that is what He's asked of them. They do it perfectly and faithfully and happily, because they love Jesus and live to serve and honor Him.

Angels can help us be better children of God, better friends of Holy Spirit, and better lovers of Jesus. What could be better than that?

What Angels Don't Have

As experienced as they are in so many areas, there are some things our angels don't know anything about. For example, they have no experience with a sin nature. Let's explore what we have in common with our beloved bodyguards as well as what we don't.

One of the biggest surprises I discovered is all the ways we are actually alike. For instance, we are created beings. That is something that we don't have in common with Jesus (Who is God), but we do have in common with angels.

But even though they are not God, and never will be, they are holy and perfect and sinless. Obviously, we are not God and we never will be, but now with our angels we have a chance to see how a created being with a free will lives in holy, sinless perfection.

Besides being sinless, angels are also not omnipotent or all powerful like God is. However, they know that He will provide whatever strength they need to accomplish the work He gives them. They don't know everything like God does either, but they know that He will give them whatever knowledge they need to succeed in their assignments.

We have this in common with angels, since we are not all knowing or all powerful, but we do have confidence God will ensure we know everything we need to know when we need to know it. We have Holy Spirit and His anointing with words of wisdom and knowledge. We also recognize that His strength is perfected in our weakness and His power within us is more than enough for any situation.

Kingdom of Joy

One way the angelic realm is different from ours is that you will never find a depressed angel. Job 38:7 says that angels shouted for joy at creation. Our angels are in a good mood because they are always in God's presence (see Matt. 18:10), and in His presence is fullness of joy (see Ps. 16:11). They rejoice over one sinner getting saved, and sinners are getting saved all the time around the world (see Luke 15:10)!

From these verses, we see that both God and His angels are happier and more fun than we may have pictured them. Angels live in Heaven where there are no tears or sin or sadness. In fact, prophetic seer Patricia King reveals that the very first time she was taken in a vision into Heaven, she heard laughter. All of Heaven was laughing! She said it was gloriously indescribable.[6] Indeed, "joy unspeakable and full of glory" is what the Bible promises (1 Pet. 1:8 KJV)!

Above all else, God wanted Patricia to experience joy and the sound of laughter in His home. What an incredible revelation of God's heart and what He values.

Angels are also different from us in that they have absolutely perfect faith in God. Their trust in Him is unwavering, and they submit to Him eagerly without hesitation. It is easy for them to have uncompromising obedience and surrender to His will because they are so intimately acquainted with His goodness, faithfulness, and love. They realize Father knows best!

The other beautiful thing about angels is that they live to worship God. They have their priorities right and never lose their focus, even for a moment. While it is a lesson many of us are still learning ourselves, angels understand their number one job, even more important than any great service or work of the Kingdom, is ministry to God. Not for Him, but to Him. And so it is with us.

Fearless

Another characteristic we immediately notice about angels is their incredibly confident nature. While completely humble, they are entirely bold and brave. They have not a hint of arrogance, but they are absolutely assured that whatever they are intending to do will be accomplished, because they have God backing them up. They don't have anything to prove to anybody; they just live to please Father.

Angels are also extraordinarily positive and give new meaning to the words *eternal optimist*! They have no fear. No pride. No stress. No doubt. It is such an awesome amalgamation, that extreme humility and extreme confidence. They have the revelation that we have won, that it is already done (see Col. 2:9-15). Jesus secured our victory and the Most High really is Ruler over the realm of mankind (see Dan. 4:17).

That version of reality is all angels see. All they know is God's truth and His perspective. The war has already been won, so they never fight *for* victory. They always, only, naturally, exclusively fight *from* a position of victory.

All of that is what we're going for. In so many ways, how they live is what we aspire to. And where else would we see an example of this— by someone who is not God Himself (Jesus)—except for in angels? We don't know anyone who is perfect. Here is our chance to see in real time what it can actually look like. Feel like. Sound like.

When we see our angels in action, we get a vision for holiness and how awesome it is, and that makes it seem a little bit more within reach. When we walk with the wise, we become wise, and if even just a tiny bit of that glory realm rubs off on us, we are a lot better off than when we started.

Who Can't Do This?

My brother's kids have all seen angels, and his middle daughter especially is a totally different girl because of it. Before Rebekah encountered angels, she used to be timid and shy, and she would choose to sit on the sidelines rather than go play with other kids. To see her now, you wouldn't believe the transformation! Today she will happily join in and make new friends at the park or visit a new children's church service— even without her siblings.

She's not afraid anymore because she sees that she's not alone. If you ask her where her guardian angels are, she will motion to either side of her. Her angels are always with her, she can always see them, and that makes all the difference in the world. She has no fear, a peaceful heart, and new confidence. That is some good fruit! And if it works for seven-year-olds, it can work for anyone.

God is infinitely creative. For as many different personalities that people have around the globe, angels also have an equally diverse range of them as well. Even my angels are not the same—they definitely have two distinct dispositions.

Angels have different roles in the Kingdom, so it makes sense that their personalities vary as well. When we consider angels, we probably most often think of warrior angels who battle and protect, like Michael (see Dan. 10:13; Rev. 12:7). However, we know there are communication specialists in the angelic realm as well, as Gabriel's primary missions involved bringing messages from God (see Dan. 9:21-23; Luke

1:19, 26-38). And of course, there are angelic worship leaders in Heaven, too (see Ps. 148:2; Rev. 5:11-13).

Just as we can be a soldier in the military, a media broadcaster on TV, or a worship leader at our church, angels have different jobs and functions as well. There is immense variety in the angelic realm, just as there is in everything God created.

Battle-Clad Warrior

For example, when my dad sees his angel, he is a giant soldier decked out in armor from head to foot. Since my father's name is Mark, which means "Strong Defender," his angel is perfectly matched to him. God realizes that since my dad is a big champion of truth, he would want to see a huge valiant warrior angel. Anything less would be a disappointment!

I am a firstborn, Type A, recovering perfectionist. That is why my angels' laidback, fun-loving, peace-keeping, joy-guarding personalities are exactly right for me. They show by example how to live and even work from a place of rest (see Heb. 4:9-11). God wants to help us maintain emotional equilibrium and bring us into balance, so He will give us whatever we need and whoever we need to get us from where we are to where He wants us to be.

Redefining Lost

To close this chapter, we will look at one last silly but sacred dream that gives us a glimpse into God's perspective on how He sees us, His angels, and their heavenly realm. First, let me fill you in on the important backstory, which is the context in which I had this dream.

After crisscrossing our third checkpoint along the US-Canadian border in under two hours, an immigration officer asked me, "Are you guys lost?" I smiled sweetly and assured him that was certainly not the case. "Oh no, sir. We're definitely not lost! We just don't know where we are in relation to where we want to be."

So we continued along our "scenic route" and eventually found ourselves where we wanted to be. The not knowing where we were simply added to the fun of the experience. I was with my brother Josh, and a friend or two were along for the ride as well. We just laughed and had a great time! We were having an adventure.

However, as much as I love having adventures, if I had been in the exact same situation all by myself, it would not have been nearly as fun. Driving around in the dark, at night, all alone, not knowing where I was going? No thanks. But as it was, with family and friends, it was a blast.

I have traveled by plane, train, and automobile. By camel, parachute, rickshaw, and bicycle-built-for-two. If there is a mode of transportation, I've probably tried it. If there is an inhabited continent, I've definitely visited it. I love exploring new places, and my favorite thing is to go where I've never been.

The best part, though, is sharing the experience, so I like to go with someone. Whether it is a girlfriend, a group of friends, my brother, or my husband—together is always much better than going it alone (see Eccl. 4:9-10). Situations that could be stressful, frustrating, or scary when I am alone become enjoyable and happy memories in the making. It just all depends on whom I'm with.

A Dream of High School

Awhile back I had been considering how I could explain the spirit realm as a fun, safe place that is wide open for great adventures. It is not foreign or scary; it is home! In that setting I had a dream.

In the dream, I went to a high school. I did not know my way around and had no idea what to do. But as soon as I arrived, I found four old friends whom I knew from a church I used to attend. They were so excited to see me again! They chatted with me, and when the bell rang, they took it upon themselves to help me get the right textbooks and escort me to the right classroom. They enthusiastically took me under their wing and made sure I was OK, which made all the difference so I wasn't anxious or stressed. It was great.

Now for most of you reading this, I imagine the idea of high school brings back some memories, fond or otherwise. That is not the case for me. Since I was homeschooled my whole life, I've actually spent more time studying Mandarin at a university in Northeast China than I have ever spent in any high school classroom in the U.S.

My point is that whatever high school may represent to you, I guarantee it does not represent that to me. High school is a very foreign place to me. It is a place I have never been, and it is totally unfamiliar. I really only know what high school is like based on what I have seen in movies or on television. It is just not part of my world.

So when I dreamed about high school, I immediately knew it was an answer to my heart's question about how to present the spirit world as a thoroughly friendly, though admittedly "foreign," place. I understand that people may not have a lot of experience being there, just like I don't have a lot of experience being in high school.

The other reason high school is the perfect picture of the spirit realm is because it is a "school of the spirit." High school is like an "above school." We are supposed to set our minds on things above. And above is up. It is not down low; it is high. So it is high school.

Our Heavenly Friends

God's message through the dream was not to worry even if we feel the spirit realm is an unfamiliar place where we are not sure what to do, because we have friends there. The friends I met in the dream were real life friends from a church I had attended called Resurrection Life Fellowship. In this dream, the emphasis was definitely on the fellowship, the friendship. It was their relationship with me that made all the difference and that transformed the potentially stressful environment into something that felt altogether navigable and safe.

In waking life, those friends represent my angels (as I told you, they "took me under their wing"). Angels escort us and help us figure out what is going on in the spirit world. Even though it might be new and unfamiliar to us, they know their way around so we can just stick with them.

The supernatural realm is their hometown, and they are more than happy to show us around. It is their pleasure to help us get the lay of the land and make sure we get a good feel for the place. They are spirits, and they very much want to share their home, the spirit realm, with us.

Kid Stuff?

Perhaps we think that because we are supposed to be grown-up sons and daughters of God that means we should be able to figure this out on our own, if we're really mature.

While it is important to be mature in Christ, here's the thing about that. My parents live in Florida, and I live in New York. When I fly down to visit them, even though I am a mature adult, they are not going to hand me a map at the airport and say, "Okay, you're on your own! Dinner's at 7:00, so try to find your way to our house by then. Good luck!"

Of course, that's not how it works. Regardless of a person's age or maturity level, when you go visit someone in their neck of the woods, they take you around. They show you some hospitality. They don't just abandon you to your own devices.

Our European Friends

Leo and I visited Estonia a few years ago, and my father has an awesome friend there with an incredibly effective drug and alcohol rehabilitation ministry called Village of Hope. Bishop Mart Vahi proudly tells people he's taught on the four keys to hearing God's voice more than anyone else in the world besides my dad!

When we went to Tallinn, Mart and his fabulous wife Alta met up with us there. They took us all around so we could catch a glimpse of the best views of the city. They shared their local dishes and desserts with us. They told us amazing stories of what God's been up to in their part of the world, and they introduced us to some of their lovely friends who lived there as well.

Because of this, even though Estonia was a totally foreign place to us—we didn't speak the language, we couldn't read the street signs—we felt totally safe. We weren't stressed at all, because they were taking care of us. They were graciously sharing their lives and their world with us. They were hosting us beautifully, in every sense of the word.

The Consummate Host

And so it is with God. He is the consummate Host. He invites us into His world when He says, "Live in the spirit. Worship in spirit. Walk in the spirit. I am Spirit, this is My home, come join Me here! You are created in My image so you are also spirit. This is your home too!"

And we go there, and it is awesome. It's not scary. It's not stressful, because we are not alone. Remember my friends from the dream who represented my guardian angels? God is showing that as we have fellowship with them, they will take good care of us. Angels will share their world with us, and this pleases God greatly.

We can trust our angels to have the gift of hospitality and believe they will watch out for us when we visit. We have been placed in their charge (see Ps. 91:11). There's no safer place to be than the presence of Jesus and His holy angels. And He is nowhere more fully expressed and perfectly known than in His spirit realm.

Sometimes, it is not so much about where we're going, as who we're going with.

What About You?

- Read Acts 8:26-40 to discover yet another way our heavenly heroes can assist us. How did God use an angel and a person to partner together for evangelism? Is it okay that Philip obeyed the angel sent to him? What was the result?

- If God gives you direction through an angel, would you listen?

- Has that ever happened?

- Would you like to have that experience?

Chapter 6

Assignment at the United Nations: Freeing the Eagle

by Joe Brock

In a previous chapter I shared about my time in the boroughs of New York City and how the Lord led me to release 2000 angels to form a diamond-shaped boundary to drain out the darkness and prevent any new evil from entering the city. This was my most recent assignment to New York City. This town has been the destination of a number of prayer trips, and I am certain there are more ahead.

Four years prior to releasing the angels in the boroughs, the Lord commissioned my daughter and me to New York City. The Lord told me in a vision I was to go and "Release the Eagle," and He revealed that this was to happen at the United Nations Building. I was not sure what He meant by "Release the Eagle," but I knew things would become clearer in time. On this trip to the United Nations I took a huge step forward in encountering and understanding the angelic.

In the fall of 2012, my oldest daughter and I headed out to New York. She was on fall break, and I was blessed and excited to have her with me all to myself. Since our children were born, we have made the reality of the spiritual life—angels, demons, visions, dreams, and hearing God's voice—a normal and natural part of their lives. There has never been a time when they did not know these things existed or how to seek God's voice. It was normal and natural to take my daughter on a trip that was prompted by a vision. We stayed in a hotel in New Jersey, and we planned out our itinerary when we arrived.

Off to the United Nations

Over the years, each prayer trip has been unique. There is always a specific and distinct desire in God's heart for what He would have me do. The locations I travel to, the exact time down to the minute I am asked to pray, and even the direction I have been required to stand or sit are all things God has led me to do.

I have often asked God why He has directed me to do specific things, but knowledge does not determine my obedience. When we trust that God knows what He is doing, it becomes easier and easier to obey. God has often revealed to me why He did what He did, but He is never required to answer to me.

Sometimes not knowing and just obeying is the safest choice. I realize that I am not equipped to know all of what God knows. There are, however, times when our amazing Father allows the eyes of our heart to see some of the things He sees. When the invisible has become visible, I have concluded that God's reality is multifaceted and we truly only see a part of it. This trip confirmed this to me once again.

My daughter and I walked through a large number of armed security personnel stationed at the entrance and into the foyer of the United Nations. There were people there from all races and nationalities, many already congregating into groups in preparation to take a tour of the building, which was also our plan.

Now at this point, I knew my assignment was to "Release the Eagle," but I still didn't know how this was going to unfold. I have learned that everything God does has a purpose and a timing. Sometimes, the insight I need comes while I am planning the itinerary of the trip, and other times He reveals the necessary details to us after we arrive at our destination. That is what happened on this mission to the United Nations.

As my daughter and I stood in our group, the Lord unexpectedly took me into an open vision where I saw a large American bald eagle wrapped multiple times in barbed wire. I heard Him say internally, but with such presence it sounded audible, "RELEASE THE EAGLE."

I knew that the Lord was commissioning me to pray and unwrap and remove the barbed wire from around the eagle. If you have ever had an experience with God like this, you will know that God can instantly download revelation with His instructions. Instead of systematically explaining things to you over time, God suddenly imparts to you a complete revelation of His plans.

As I saw this large eagle wrapped in barbed wire, God revealed that I was to pray in intervals to release the eagle from its entrapment. I also understood that the eagle represented the United States and that God was releasing our country from a painful bondage. God was declaring freedom over the United States by removing the bondage, and by His mercy and grace I was to be a part of this deliverance.

A Divine Change-up

As I wrapped my head around the commission God had given me, the tour guide introduced herself and slipped away for a few minutes before the tour started. Little did I know, but God was divinely setting us up for a unique experience. I thought my only purpose on this trip was to release the eagle, but in a few moments I was about to experience one of the most exciting and mind-expanding escapades to date.

When our tour guide returned, she was surprised to announce that our tour would include a special stop to the Security Council room. We were the first group to be allowed to see the Security Council room that day. The stop was added to our tour in honor of a Muslim holiday occurring on the following day. When you walk with God, the phrase "You are not going to believe this" becomes one of your favorites.

> But Jesus looked at them and said, "With man this is impossible, but with God all things are possible. (Matthew 19:26 ESV)

I am positive that none of us fully understand just how in control God truly is. There are times when the United Nations tour includes a visit to the Security Council. On this particular day, however, it was not scheduled. Then, just minutes before we were to begin the tour, the person in charge called our tour guide over to instruct her to take us to the Council Chamber. God had this set up all along. When you walk with God and something unexpected happens, seek the Spirit and intensify your focus on Him, because God is about to astound you.

Waving Back and Forth to Angels

The tour guide led our group into the room where the International Security Council meets to maintain peace and security on a global scale. We were seated on stadium type seats. Each chair had a headset that enabled delegates and visitors to hear a translation of the council meetings.

My daughter sat down to my right. As we were settling in to hear the tour guide speak, *I saw them.* Along the back wall of the room is a very large mural. Standing shoulder-to-shoulder in front of the mural were angels—large, beautiful angels.

As I sat there, I allowed the moment to sink in. There, across the room from me was a series of huge, fascinatingly clothed angelic beings. In the council room, there is a horseshoe-shaped table surrounded by chairs. Based on the size of the chairs and the people that would sit in them, I estimated that the angels were between eight and nine feet tall. This is when things truly began to turn supernatural.

As I studied the angels, it was clear that each angel represented a certain part of the world. Their spiritual skin color and clothing reflected this. The first angel to the far left was black in color and was dressed like an African warrior from years ago. He held a large diamond-shaped shield in his right hand that was as tall as he was and a spear in his left hand that was at least a foot taller than he was.

To his left was an angel Caucasian in appearance. He was the same physical size as the African-looking angel. However, this angel was dressed in an old U.S. Army uniform from the Korean War era. The clothing looked like the uniforms on the television show M.A.S.H. I do remember one more angel in a Scottish kilt, but that is all I confidently recall.

At this moment, I leaned over and whispered to my daughter to tell her that there were angels standing in front of us along the back wall. As I told her this, I remained visually focused on the angels and pointed in their direction. Then it happened.

When I pointed at the angels, I made direct eye contact with the one dressed like he was in the American military. As I whispered to my daughter, I realized this angel was aware of my awareness of him. In a look of bewilderment, he raised his right arm slightly and subtly waved at me with small back-and-forth gestures. He looked like he was trying to wave inconspicuously, and he kept his arm close to his torso while he waved.

I sat back in my chair while maintaining eye contact with the angel. I then flashed him a big smile and waved back in the same manner he was waving at me. He realized I could see him, and his whole spiritual demeanor was that of amazement and intrigue. His eyes widened in surprise, and we just waved back and forth for a couple of seconds.

I was still smiling when he turned and tapped the African warrior angel to his right. I watched him lean over to whisper to the other angel as he pointed to me. The African warrior angel then looked directly at me and he also waved at me.

This angel had the same reaction; he was in shock and awe. They stood there almost looking giddy, as they continued to smile and wave at me. I was delighted to oblige and wave back. Because of the interaction I had with these two angels, I never really focused in on the others. What an exhilarating experience!

Studying Angels versus Experiencing Them

Pondering this encounter over the years, I have found the answers to my questions leading to more questions. Reading the Bible and establishing a safe, theological foundation about the angelic is absolutely necessary. The Bible is not, however, a book that tells us to read it and then stop there. No, the Bible demands we become doers of the Word (see James 1:22); it is a book of experiences. The Bible's purpose is to give us a paradigm of how to act, behave, and be, according to the nature of God.

The Bible demonstrates angels have limited power, authority and understanding. In Scripture, angels are instructed and assigned tasks. When I saw the angels in the council room, I actually saw and watched their behavior. I know that seeing a person for a few minutes cannot possibly explain all there is to know about them. This holds true to the angelic realm as well. I have not learned everything about angels—I'm not even close. I have, however, learned a few things.

For example, I realized they did not know I was aware of them until I let them know I could see them. Once I did, they responded with varying emotions—excitement, surprise, and joy. There was an undeniable connection we shared, even if it only lasted a few moments.

Their attire indicated that there was a correlation between the geographic locations they spiritually represented and what they were wearing. I also sensed that the time period of their clothing indicated how long they had been in the Security Council room. The United Nations building was completed in 1952, which corresponded with the garments the angels wore. I wonder if the Lord sent a believer to this newly constructed building in 1952 to release these angels to watch over the global affairs that would transpire in this room. I will find out for sure in Heaven.

I find myself wondering how deep a relationship humans and angels can have. I also wonder what we would see if God were to fully pull back the veil between the spiritual and the physical. Was I the only human to ever see the angels standing there? These are wonderful thoughts to have. Again, in Heaven (hopefully sooner) I will find out.

Time to Release the Eagle

Once we left the council room, we made our way through the building continuing our tour. Our guide talked about the purpose and history of the United Nations. At certain points along the tour, the Lord would spontaneously reopen the vision of the eagle wrapped in barbed wire and prompt me to pray. Each time I saw the eagle, there was progressively less wire wrapped around it.

At the end of the tour, I had one last vision of the eagle. This time there was no barbed wire around it, and I sensed it had no injuries. I knew in my spirit that God was telling me to release the eagle. My daughter and I moved away from the crowds of people and found a quiet spot. In this place of stillness, I held the eagle's body in my hands facing away from me.

In the vision, I lifted my hands up to release the bird and audibly (yet quietly) told the eagle it was free. As this was happening in the vision, I moved my hands as if I were releasing an eagle as a prophetic gesture. In the vision, I saw the eagle flap its wings, and it majestically flew away.

Something Extra

Before I move on, I feel the Lord wants me to share something else He showed me that day. One of the stops along the tour was the United Nations General Assembly Hall. You may have seen this large room in pictures, and it seats the 193 international delegates.

The moment we walked in as a group, I could see in the spiritual realm God standing on the main stage hunched over the podium area because He was so tall. I was seeing not the Father, or the Son, or the Spirit specifically. Instead, I saw the glorious godhead—the Trinity—at the podium.

The ceiling of the room is 75 feet high. God was so tall that He was hunched over the podium and His shoulder blades touched the ceiling. If He had stood erect, He would have easily been head and shoulders taller than the ceiling.

I was also immediately aware of the spiritual climate of the room. As you grow more sensitive to the spirit realm, you begin to discern changes in the spiritual atmosphere. Our physical bodies can sense the temperature, wind, and humidity. When the physical atmosphere around you changes, your outer man is aware of it. Your inner man is just as aware of changes in the spirit realm as your outer man is towards physical things. When I walked in the room, my spirit man was aware of an atmosphere I had never felt before.

Over the years, I (like many others) have grown in my desire to know what is happening in the spiritual more than the natural. What is happening in the spiritual is true reality and acts as the precursor to what will happen and manifest in the natural.

As I am writing this, I am sitting at a local library. As soon I walked in, I immediately began sensing and looking for what was happening in the spirit realm throughout the library. I often feel a spiritual darkness in libraries due to the nature of the books and what spiritual doors they may open. The great thing about our salvation is Jesus empowers us to take authority over the enemy. As soon as I sensed the darkness in the library, I took authority over it.

In situations like this, I place spiritual restrictions on the demonic in the heavenly places and in the facilities themselves and deny them the right to broadcast their evil. I also have learned to release angels to stand guard and create a spiritual barrier around me as I work. As I found a place to sit in the library, I took authority over the darkness and in no time the atmosphere changed and I was able to work in an anointed spiritual environment.

This is what happened when I walked into the General Assembly room. I began discerning in my spirit, but I felt nothing, as if there was a spiritual vacuum that was void of anything. This was completely foreign to me.

As we were being seated, I immediately began asking the Lord what was happening and what was I sensing. As I sought Him, He drew my attention back to Him standing bent over on the main stage. He began talking to me about the room we were in and what it represented. He said that global decisions were made in this room that affected everyone on the earth.

Then He said that the majority of the people that make these decisions are not anti-God; He said that they are simply incognizant to His existence. They believe that *they* are in control of reality and that *they* are the one's making the global decisions. They are blinded and deceived, but He is always fully in charge.

I understood then why He stood towering over the stage and group. He is much greater than all of the world's leaders and decision makers. He is truly in charge, despite the fact He is not always acknowledged. The feeling of spiritual nothingness was the manifestation of the global human attitude toward the existence of God. In the world's eyes, God is nothing. There is a lack of awareness of His existence. This made the world much smaller to me. The world is big, but God was undeniably bigger.

God's Amazing Confirmations

With our mission at the United Nations Building completed, it was time to prepare for our return home. After I complete a mission, I always look and pray for confirmations that we were accurate and obedient to God's will. It can be daunting to have multiple visions, hear God's voice with such clarity, and see angels smile and wave at you! I sometimes wonder and have doubts about what I see and do. God is so faithful though—He knows my weakness at these times and has been gracious to supernaturally reassure me. This trip was no exception.

The hotel where my daughter and I had stayed was on a very, very busy stretch of road and when you pulled out, you had to accelerate as fast as possible to avoid an accident. As we were leaving the hotel for the last time, we had to sit there with the traffic speeding by for a few moments waiting for a chance to exit. Our time came, and I floored it, accelerating quickly to make it safely onto the road. It was a harrowing moment and we were both relieved when we made it. As we approached the traffic in front of us that had stopped at the light, we pulled up behind a very large pickup truck. I glanced at our surroundings and eventually looked back at the truck in front of me. This is the moment we saw God's confirmation.

There were 30-40 stickers all over the back of the truck with pictures of the American eagle and the letters USA! My daughter and I smiled at each other as God confirmed that yes, we truly saw what we saw and our mission to help liberate our nation by breaking the bondage off the eagle and releasing it was complete. God truly does more than our minds can comprehend and our hearts can desire.

Jesus, Our Example

It is my prayer that you are inspired and provoked to hunger for these things in your life. I encourage you to prayerfully reread your Bible under the illumination of the Holy Spirit, asking Him to lead and guide you into all truth concerning the angelic. Jesus was ministered to by angels, and they minister to us as well.

Then the devil left him, and behold, angels came and were ministering to him. (Matthew 4:11)

Are they not all ministering spirits sent out to serve for the
sake of those who are to inherit salvation? (Hebrews 1:14)

Do you notice there is ambiguity in how the angels ministered to Jesus? The Bible never tells us *how* they served Him. The same is true with the Hebrews passage. All the Bible tells us is that they *will* serve us, the redeemed of Christ. It never specifies how.

My belief is that if the biblical authors had been more specific in what the angels did in these passages, we would limit ourselves to just their behaviors in these scriptural instances. However, by being purposely obscure, this allows God the freedom to utilize the angels to serve us in unlimited ways. If the Bible purposefully does not define the role of angels in our lives, like in these biblical accounts, we should allow the Holy Spirit great latitude in His dealing with us.

In upcoming chapters, I will share how angels served and helped me fulfill the purposes of God. As you prayerfully meditate on what the Bible says about the angelic and insert yourself into these narratives, see yourself as the beneficiary of these spiritual beings. Accept that they are involved in your life right now. God wants to open the eyes of your heart to see and interact with them.

If you know Jesus, the Bible plainly says that angels are there for you. This is why we are writing this book—not to fascinate you with our stories, but to inspire you to connect with God so you can experience them for yourself.

What About You?

What did you think about the Security Council room suddenly being opened to us? Have you ever had something unexpected like this happen as God ordered your steps? What was your experience?

- Have you ever had a vision? What kind of experiences have you had seeing in the spirit?

- Read Luke 22:43. Who was the angel strengthening? Does this surprise you? Has this ever happened in your life?

- If God sent an angel to strengthen you, how would you react?

Chapter 7

Living with Angels: Real-Time Conversations and Reality Checks

by Charity Kayembe

One day Pojes happily sighed, "Jesus and Father just love you so much! They talk about you all the time."

Another day Shobis encouraged me, "Don't worry, Milady, Father's got a plan. He always has a plan!"

Still another time they told me, "We love being about Father's business with you."

Finally, I couldn't ignore it anymore. I said, "Guys, I'm really not trying to be rude or mean or anything, but...God is *my* Dad. I mean, where do you get off calling Him 'Father' all the time? No offense, but I thought He was my Father, not yours..."

I am grateful that angels are not easily insulted!

Father of All

Pojes was quick to clarify my thinking. "Uh...yeah. Actually, He's totally our Father, too. Just because we work for Him doesn't mean God the Father doesn't treat us well, with love and respect, and even like a dad. He can be our boss and our dad at the same time. You know from personal experience how that is!

"Yes, He's the Commander of our Angelic Hosts, but at the same time, He loves and cares about us. He IS love, remember? So there is no separation between who He cares a lot about and a little about. He just cares. He just loves!

"...That is actually why we never felt the need to rebel and leave here. What's not to love about such an amazing arrangement? It's like Heaven... ha-ha, oh wait, it IS Heaven..."

Oh brother!

I still felt unsure about all of this, but not long after that exchange Holy Spirit drew my attention to Job 38:4-7. The passage talks about creation and who was around when God made everything. Obviously, we weren't there (nor was Job, which was God's point). But then it says who was there—and that these "sons of God shouted for joy" (Job 38:7 ESV).

In fact, *throughout* Job, that's how angels are consistently identified: sons of God.

Creator-Father

Who created me? My dad and mom. Who created you? Your dad and mom. Whoever creates you is your father and mother. So, in that sense, God is easily seen as the Father of angels, since He created them. He's their Creator-Father.

In *Angels: Elect & Evil*, C. Fred Dickason writes:

> Each angel is a direct creation from God, for they do not procreate as do humans (Matt. 22:28-30). Perhaps this is why they are sometimes called 'the sons of God' (Job 1:6, 2:1). The word 'sons' seems to indicate a direct creation of God, as Adam is the 'son of God' (Lk. 3:38), and believers are recreated in Christ individually as 'sons of God' (Gal. 3:26).[7]

It's true that God created me and knit me together in my mother's womb. It's also true that God created Adam and Eve. And then they had kids, who had kids, who eventually had my parents, who had me. So I am quite removed from that initial Adam and Eve creation by God.

Angels aren't, though. Every angel is like an Adam and Eve creation, in that every single individual angel is a direct, personal, hands-on creation of God. He put His thought and time and creative energy and love into each and every one of them.

That is a lot of caring for a lot of angels. How could I not care about them, too?

Obviously, angels are not sons of God the way Jesus is *the* Son of God, and Jesus is God Himself. Nor are angels children of God like we are. As Christians, we received the DNA of God (see 1 Pet. 1:23). We have the supernatural genes of the Almighty flowing through us (see 2 Pet. 1:4). But God loves relationship and family, and He has other angelic "sons" for us to work together with in His Kingdom. He is creator of everything and Father of all (see Eph. 4:6).

Who's Your Daddy?

Interestingly enough, before I learned all this, my niece Rebekah and I were discussing our angelic guardians. As soon as I mentioned my angels' names, she immediately and excitedly assumed they were siblings. Well, that thought had never crossed my mind!

Now, Bekah is a spiritual dynamo, but she was also seven at the time of this conversation. Of course, I didn't want to look down on her youth, but at the same time I really didn't know what to do with her intuitive understanding and revelation about our heavenly friends.

But now that I see what the Bible says, I think she's right. We know even anthropologically speaking that a sibling is simply another member of a unilateral descent group sharing kinship through a mutual ancestor. No wonder I always get a sibling vibe from them! My Father's sons are angels, and we all share the same Dad.

Jesus' Side of the Tracks

That revelation was huge and took me some time to fully wrap my heart around. God patiently continued to unpack dimensions of it though, until I finally began to see things from His point of view.

When I was younger, I misunderstood Father's heart on the angelic realm. If you had brought it up, I would have told you "I'm just not that into angels." It wasn't that I had anything against them; it's just that they are not God. Father? He's my Life. Jesus? The Lover of my soul. Holy Spirit? My best Friend. The Trinity—I'm all about them! Give me *God*.

But angels? They were more of a side dish, an accessory. Like an opening act of some kind. The Trinity is who I really care about. Who is better than God? Who is bigger than God? Nobody is more awesome and worthy and incredible than Him, right?

True, true, and true.

But then Jesus, Who is Truth Himself, gave me His version of Truth which was even more true than my truth.

THE GAME-CHANGER

Jesus said: "Charity, how would you feel if, when you were getting to know Leo and you invited him to meet your family, he said, 'No thanks. I'm not really into your family; I'm just into you.'

"Or what if every time you invited him to hang out with your friends, he declined, explaining how much he totally loved you and just wanted to focus on you and you alone? What if he wanted to be with you exclusively, but never wanted to be with your friends?"

Well, if Leo didn't want to meet my family, didn't want to come to my house, my neighborhood, have dinner with my parents, or hang out with my friends at least some of the time, I would take serious issue with that. He may love me, but he would not be very good at showing it.

If Jesus had homeboys, who would they be?

And so it is with me. How can I say I love Jesus and not care about what and who is important to Him? Why should I insist that He always has to come to me and get into my world? Shouldn't I sometimes go over to His side of the tracks, spend time in His neighborhood, get to know His family, and hang out with His friends?

Angels, these *sons of God* that they are, have been a part of Jesus' life since before time began. As my angels clarified for me: Jesus is Love, and there's really no off switch for that. He cannot love me a lot and then love them a little or someone else not at all. He just loves. And there's more than enough for all of us.

What Love Does

Now that Jesus explained His perspective, I was finally getting the revelation. Now I will purpose to spend time in the spirit realm with

Him and His angels. I will "draw near to Him" by choosing to go where He is and meet Him there. And I will get to know everyone in His world.

Because angels are important to Him, they are important to me.

Because I care about Jesus, and because that's just what love does.

The Day I Couldn't See My Angels

Once I began loving not only Jesus, but also everyone in His world, I became accustomed to fellowship with His company of Heaven often. Then the unexpected happened.

I had traveled out of town and was in another city. The first morning I was away, I woke up early and immediately attempted to engage the supernatural realm. I wanted to connect with Jesus and my angels. The only problem was that I couldn't see any of them.

What was going on? Is it because I'm in a different place? Can I not discern as clearly here? I know they are with me, so why can't I see them?

You can imagine my relief when two familiar friendly faces shifted into view.

"Hey, where have you guys been? What's going on here?"

Poje motioned with his head over in Jesus' and Father's direction.

"They don't want you to see us easily, because then you'll feel obliged to engage us in conversation."

I scrunched up my nose and raised an eyebrow doubtfully, glancing at Shobi. Surprisingly, he agreed.

"It's true, Milady. Father knows what you need most right now is sleep. You've had a short night and they want you to get more rest. Sweet dreams...now go back to bed!"

Distracted by Heaven

Well, that worked for me. I had crawled into bed just a few hours before, and I was still exhausted. So I promptly rolled over and fell back asleep. Later that morning when I woke up again, this time refreshed and well-rested, I reflected back on our conversation. It was only then that I began to realize what their words actually meant. And it was awesome.

We live in a world of singing cell phones, pinging text messages, email notifications, tweets, status updates, radios, and TVs blaring everywhere. We literally have non-stop pulls on our attention in a hundred different directions at once. I need to go out of my way, regularly, to create a space of quiet. I must be intentional and relentless in my pursuit of a place of peace.

Jesus didn't have any of these 21st century distractions, yet He still made it a point to get away. To go to the lonely places. The quiet places. The wilderness and the mountains where He could get away from everything that would disrupt His focus on the spirit realm and communion with Father.

How much more so do we? I do my best to minimize the incessant barrage of superficial diversions from ultimate Kingdom reality. I continuously endeavor to look past the natural realm noise and quiet down so I can clearly pick up on the signals of the spirit. Usually (and when I say usually, I mean always) it had been that this physical world was a distraction to my focused intention on the supernatural.

But all of a sudden, now it is the opposite. God was saying He didn't want me to see my angels in the spirit realm at that moment, because then I would be distracted from what I should be doing in the physical realm (letting myself sleep).

This means that with practiced focus it's possible for the supernatural world to become so real that it could distract us from the physical world. Now that's what we're talking about. Living in such a way that we are actually distracted by Heaven? Bring it on!

Angelic Bodyguards

Psalm 91 is a powerful passage about our heavenly protection and reveals another aspect of God's design for angels and what they are up to in our lives.

> *He will give His angels charge concerning you,*
> *to guard you in all your ways.*
> *They will bear you up in their hands,*
> *that you do not strike your foot against a stone.* (Psalm 91:11-12)

What an incredible promise! A natural picture to help us understand this blessing even more in our everyday lives would be the analogy of babysitting my niece. We have a stream near our house so imagine we went for a walk along the edge of it together, hand in hand. She's in my charge. I am responsible for her, and it is my job to protect her.

As we walk along the stream, side by side, she begins to stumble towards the water and "strike her foot against a stone." Well, I can help prevent that. Because her hand is in mine, I can easily pull her up and protect her. She doesn't fall because she's close to me. We are walking together.

And so it is with our guardian angels.

They are close to us, walking together with us, and they are able to keep us from falling. Daniel 4:13 says that angels are holy watchers. They watch out for us! We are in their charge so it is their responsibility to protect us. And as we purpose to live in step with them, we make their job that much easier.

This passage in Psalms also tells us that angels guard us in all our ways. All means all, so we certainly don't want to limit what they can or cannot do for us. God will use His angels in the most creative and surprising ways, as illustrated in the next story. If nothing else, life with angels is anything but boring!

Fanning the Flame

As mentioned, one of the most delightful characteristics of angels is their irrepressibly optimistic nature. They are never brought down by our bad attitudes and instead do everything in their power to encourage and bless us. This truth was really brought home for me one particular day when I was not in a very good mood and knew I needed to have a quiet time. While the company of Heaven always cheers me up, at that moment they definitely had their work cut out for them!

I didn't even bother to sit up, but leaned across the couch, closing my eyes and looking for God to show me something that would refresh my tired soul and body. All of a sudden, Pojes and Shobis came into focus, and they were waving palm branches. These were the really big kind of branches, the ones that might be used in a king's palace.

And they started fanning me with them.

I wasn't sure that was a very spiritual thing for them to be doing and, of course, I let them know. They continued their elaborate fanning display, however, patiently reminding me of Second Timothy 1:6. Pojes winked at Shobis and could no longer keep a straight face. He finally explained, "Don't you get it, Milady? We're fanning the flame within you!" And with that they both burst out laughing at their own little joke.

Somehow that was never quite what I pictured when I read that verse and I laughed too at the fun version of this Scripture that I was now living. And just like that, my angelic guardians had once again successfully protected my peace and restored my joy. Watching over my heart is their specialty, and they are very good at what they do.

God's Heart

This experience demonstrates again how much God cares about our emotional wellbeing. I used to think that as long as I was doing the right things then it was not a big deal if I was stressed or overwhelmed in the midst of it. All that mattered was that I was obeying the Bible and accomplishing ministry work.

As I have mentioned, Holy Spirit really turned this around for me and has shown me that how we feel matters a lot to our heavenly Father. Peace and joy are not just nice feelings. They are, in fact, the very Kingdom of God (see Rom. 14:17). How can I advance His Kingdom of peace and joy when I'm not living in peace and joy?

The degree that we are overwhelmed and not experiencing peace and rest is the degree that we are not living into His Kingdom. If we allow fear in our hearts, then we are not inside God's heart, as He is love and perfect love drives out fear. If we are not joyful, then we are not aware and living to the truth that He is with us, because in His presence is fullness of joy (see Ps. 16:11).

I love how the "Joy Apostle" Georgian Banov explains the importance of these holy emotions in *Angel Stories*:

> Joy is a spiritual frequency the demonic cannot stand. They cannot sustain themselves in it. It has a crippling and maddening effect on them. Satan does not like to be mocked, so laughter is the last thing he wants to hear from

us. So joy is a very, very powerful element, and I always aim to break into the level of joy at which it breaks out and the heavens are released. Heaven is full of joy! I want to connect with that joy.[8]

We see then how checking in on our emotional state is a great way to gauge if we are living in the Kingdom the way Father desires, experiencing His heart of love and the fruit of His Spirit in our lives: joy, peace, and faith.

I am thankful that when I get out of balance, Father uses His ministering spirits, my angels, to bring me around again (see Heb. 1:14). They always make me laugh! They know me well and knew that their flame-fanning antics would put me in a much better place emotionally and spiritually. Indeed, a joyful heart is good medicine (see Prov. 17:22)!

I am so grateful for a God who cares about our feelings and is so gentle and playful and kind. And I am grateful for the supernatural guardians He's entrusted us to, for they protect us in all ways (see Ps. 91:11). They not only protect our physical body, but they also watch over our heart and soul as well.

God has given His angels charge over us. What does that look like? You never know—some days it just might involve a bit of unexpected flame-fanning, and some really big palm branches.

What About You?

- Are you ready to visit Jesus' family on the other side of the tracks? Have you? What was your experience?

- Read 2 Kings 6:15-17 and Ephesians 1:18. Did you ever notice the similarities in Elisha and Paul's prayers? How often do you pray this for yourself? What have been the results?

- When have you been aware that an angel was watching over you and keeping you safe? What happened?

- Spend some time thanking God for the heavenly bodyguards He has assigned to you.

Chapter 8

Washington, DC:
Explosion in the Heavenlies Part I

by Joe Brock

My son and I spent time sightseeing in Washington D.C. before we arrived in New York to release angels in the boroughs. As we traveled around the city, God started opening the eyes of my heart to see the spiritual reality that exists throughout our current political system. He gave me wisdom and understanding and insights about the city.

As my son and I drove the streets of our capital, God acted as my teacher. It always fascinates me when God begins teaching you something without an immediate context. I have learned to trust that there is always a specific reason for the lessons, even if that reason isn't obvious to you at the time. You may not recognize it at the moment, but in time things become apparent. God is not arbitrary and He has a purpose in every decision He makes. While we were driving through the streets of D.C., looking at the different buildings and tourist sites, God began opening my eyes.

Grids and Paradigms

All of us have grids or paradigms. A paradigm is a systematic way we each look at and then interpret the reality we daily engage in. Our perception is the sum accumulation of how all of our teachings, experiences, and interactions have molded us into who we are and what we believe. This happens through parents, teachers, friends, enemies, and even the demonic.

All of our life experiences, successes, and pains blend together to create a lens that heavily influences how we react to and interpret the world around us. Your favorite sports team is often your parent's favorite team. Your view on social issues, religion, and money is strongly affected by the people around you, the home you were raised in, and the friends you have. I am no exception.

Most of us do not know what we believe until something or someone with a contradictory or challenging view engages us. There is seldom any reason to examine what we think so long as we live the same predictable daily life. However, growth often comes when what we believe is forced to be inspected; this can be both a terrifying and liberating thing.

At this time in my life, my paradigm of government was something very high and lofty. The idea of the Department of Education, the Department of Defense, or the Department of Justice was too big for me to wrap my head around. These large agencies that influence laws, people's lives, and billions of dollars was beyond my mental grasp—until the Holy Spirit began opening my eyes.

You almost need to be a seer to find a parking place in the center of Washington, DC! My son and I wanted to visit the Lincoln Memorial, so we drove up and down numerous side streets looking for a place to park. We finally found an open spot across the street from the underground garage of an agency building where two armed guards controlled who came in and out.

As we got out of our car to pay the meter, one of the guards hollered that we were not allowed to park there. There was a sign just in front of us that said this street was temporarily closed to non-governmental vehicles. We thanked him and got back in the car. It was while we were sitting there, trying to determine our next course of action, that the Holy Spirit began pulling back the veil and revealed the spirit realm to me.

Opening My Eyes

As we sat there, I watched numerous men and women entering and exiting this large government building. They were different heights, different races, and different ages, but all had a special badge that allowed them the freedom to enter. As I watched this for a minute or so, God began to reveal to me the real nature and reality of politics. The significant buildings, government agencies, and political hob-knobbing, they all boil down to one simple word—*thoughts*.

Over the last few years, much has been written on the power of our thoughts. What we believe is perhaps the most significant factor in how we live, act, and react. When you stop and consider the basis of politics, it all comes down to one simple fact—people believe certain things to be true, and when they feel their view is vital, they seek to influence others to that same perception. They want others to believe as they do. This is how politics work.

God began allowing me to see that there were demons on the backs of many of these people. Also, bear in mind that what God was showing me at this single agency represented politics as a whole. This particular agency was one of the hundreds throughout D.C. So, I believe this means that in every agency, there are demons that have fastened themselves to the backs of people that work there.

This is a demonic attempt to plant evil thoughts in people and see them grow into full belief systems. It does not stop there, however. The demonic realm convinces a person that their beliefs are good and true, and that it is imperative to share them with others.

Each time this seed of darkness is sown into another's mind, this idea potentially spreads. As the idea spreads, and more people accept it, it gains more cultural credibility. Eventually, enough people believe it, and through the political system, it is introduced as a potential law. If the law is voted on and becomes established, this law then has jurisdiction over people.

This is how evil propagates: a single, evil thought planted in people grows and deceives until it becomes established as law. There are people the demonic has targeted in every sector of life to use them as carriers of evil thoughts. The demonic will also give these people great prestige and authority and make them seem larger than life for the sole purpose of winning over the masses. Hitler is a good example of this.

We sat there watching the coming and going of numerous politicians. Eventually, we drove away, but not before I had received this spiritual insight into politics. I was able to see the power of how a single thought could grow into a governing law. What seemed like a high and lofty idea—government—was now simple and easy to perceive.

Along with this, the Lord showed me that these people were not intrinsically evil; they were deceived. They genuinely believe that certain things like abortion, a person getting to determine what gender they want to be, and homosexuality as a biblically approved lifestyle are virtuous and right.

They believe this because a single thought entered their mind and, without something to counter it, made its way into their heart until it grew and took over their worldview. We need to love them, not hate them. I want my own deception to be prayed for, not preyed upon. Therefore, we must treat others as we want to be treated.

After a few hours of sightseeing, and receiving amazing revelation form the Lord, the time arrived for my son and me to leave Washington, D.C. and head to the boroughs of New York. As we exited the city, my son made a general statement that turned out to be prophetic: "You know Dad, it would be a lot easier just to fly here than to drive all these miles."

The Holy Spirit gave me an internal reaction to what he said, which caused me to focus on it for a few minutes. We arrived in New York, but this statement never left my mind. Shortly after returning home, I understood why.

Quick Turn Around

Once we were back in Indiana, I spent time spiritually debriefing with the Lord about the trip. I always spend time praying and pondering before the Lord to ensure I completed His mission. When the confirmation comes, I am then able to move on to what God has next.

It was during this time of debriefing that the Lord told me I would be going back to Washington. This was the fastest turnaround for another trip I'd ever had, and my son's statement was actually a word from God. Just eleven days after returning from Washington, D.C. and New York City, I flew back on assignment. For this mission, the clock was ticking.

As I debriefed with the Lord about New York City, He began speaking to me about Washington, D.C. As He spoke, He identified a specific institution in D.C. that carried some of the vilest ideas ever to enter our nation. The Lord told me that I would be traveling back to D.C. and would physically go to this location. While there, I would walk around the building on the sidewalks and pour anointing oil as inconspicuously as possible. As I did this, I was to confess and repent of the sins born from this place and let the power of the Blood of Jesus remove all that God intended. I have done this many times. Each time, however, God does something unique that I have never seen before. This trip was no different.

The day arrived for me to go. My flight was booked out of Indianapolis, Indiana and no one knew about this trip except my wife and me. There are times when being discreet is a good thing. Slipping in, doing what needs to be done, and slipping out in secret has served me well.

When I arrived at the airport, there was no parking for blocks and blocks. By the time I made it to the terminal, I was five minutes late and was put on standby. It is easy to say that God is in control, but moments like this test us, and we must choose to remain in peace, confident that God's sovereignty is not just a word but an absolute reality.

I found a place to sit, had breakfast, and patiently waited. Missing the flight created an additional problem; I had rented a car for only a few hours. I was supposed to arrive in D.C. early in the morning, pick up the car, go to my destination, and be back quickly to catch my flight home. When I eventually did arrive in D.C., I was already running behind. Again, it is at times like this you must encourage yourself to trust that the Lord knows what He is doing.

Time to Pray

I picked up the vehicle and used the GPS on my phone to navigate through D.C. to my appointed location. I circled the building a couple of times to get my bearings. I found a place to park close enough to walk to the facility.

After a couple of minutes in prayer, I exited the car and proceeded to the west side of the building until I reached the rear of the location. Up to this point, I had no awareness of anything supernatural. I had no visions or prophetic words from the Lord. I was just walking in obedience. As I walked alongside the front of the building, I did the most powerful thing a Christian can do: I began confessing, repenting, and asking for forgiveness for any sin that was committed in this place that would open the door to the darkness, through the Atonement of Christ.

As I was doing this, I took some anointing oil out and started pouring a few drops on the ground every few feet. As I approached the entrance of the building, two armed female security guards came out to have a cigarette. Picture this: I am walking alone in front of a globally recognized political institution and systemically pouring anointing oil on the ground. If my behavior raises any type of alarm, I would be asked to explain myself. How would I answer this? "I am a minister of the Gospel from Indiana here to pour oil on the ground and repent for the sins and atrocities committed in this building." If I said that, I might not make it home for dinner.

What I did was begin scratching my right ankle, which was on the opposite side from the women. Each time I knelt down to scratch, I poured oil out on the ground at an angle they could not see. I also struck up a conversation with them. For the time of the year, it happened to be an exceptionally warm day. I kept them talking about the weather as I passed by, and I finally arrived at the end of the building.

By this time they reentered the facility, and I then stopped and turned around—and that is when it happened.

Pushing the Plunger and Angels Arrive

As I turned around, I had an open vision of a large, older looking brick building about 40 feet in front of me. The bricks were a worn orange and the mortar in between them was a discolored white. Then, an angel suddenly appeared in front of me and handed me a bomb detonator. It was the plunger-type square box with a handle on top that is pulled upward and then pushed down. He never spoke, but I knew I was supposed to use it.

Keep in mind that I am standing in a public place looking in the spirit realm at this large brick building with an angel handing me a detonator device and expecting me to use it. Scripture records that there are physical gestures we can do in the natural realm that have prophetic, spiritual consequences (see 1 Sam. 15:27-28; Acts 21:10-11). Discretion is something I have learned on these trips. It's a real skill to do what God is telling you to do in such a way you do not attract attention.

As I looked around nonchalantly to ensure no one was looking, I physically pulled the plunger up and then back down into the box. Without warning, there was an explosion in the spirit realm I cannot adequately describe. I was not at all prepared for what I witnessed. The brick building exploded in all areas and in all parts. Debris from the building was landing all around me in the spiritual realm.

There was so much dust in the spirit realm that I realized I could not see all that had happened in the explosion. The dust began to settle allowing me a clearer vision of where this building once stood. As the dust dissipated, I started seeing angels all through the bricks and mortar. Some of the angels were picking up the bricks while two specific angels were working together to pick up a large piece of the building to remove it.

As I watched this, the angels quickly removed the debris down to the ground. Then, I saw angels arrive with brooms and dustpans to sweep up all the rubble so all evidence of the building was gone. There was no sign of it at all.

The angels reminded me of a construction crew that worked in phases. Each phase of angels knew precisely what to do. There was no banter between them. There was no talk or communication. Each angel came at the time it needed to and did only the work it seemed to be assigned to do. When a particular angel did what it was supposed to do, I could no longer see it. I did not actually watch it leave; the angel seemed just to do its task and then was no longer visible. This was a fantastic sight to behold.

A Single Thought Is Like a Single Seed—Good or Bad

Here is my summation of what I saw happen. God taught me the power of how a single thought can grow into an actual, manifested reality. The single thought of abortion, for example, has grown to the point it has become law. Some of the most evil and grotesque thoughts have originated in the building to which I was sent. These ideas infiltrated the minds of the people who worked in this building and eventually became laws that govern our land. This kind of thinking not only allows for these types of ungodly beliefs, but they attract others with the same ideology.

The orange building was a demonic stronghold that has systematically grown over the years. According to Scripture, a stronghold is a fortified place in the spiritual realm where evil thoughts have evolved into an established belief system. When we are called to destroy a stronghold, we are being invited to terminate a demonic-based thinking pattern that exists in the heavens. Paul says it like this:

> *For though we walk in the flesh, we are not waging war according to the flesh. For the weapons of our warfare are not of the flesh but have divine power to destroy strongholds. We destroy arguments, and every lofty opinion raised against the knowledge of God and take every thought captive to obey Christ, being ready to punish every disobedience, when your obedience is complete* (2 Corinthians 10:3-6 ESV).

There is not the time to thoroughly discuss this here, but the demonic is bound to darkness. Sin is seen as spiritual darkness (see Acts 26:18). The way to remove the darkness is by confessing sin to the Lord Jesus and allowing His cleansing blood to remove the sin. As the sin is being eliminated, the power the enemy derives from the darkness becomes smaller until the enemy has no power or legal right to remain.

As I confessed on behalf of the people who were in the building, God removed the enemy's right to be there. This is what ultimately gave me the authority to push the plunger and destroy the stronghold that was there. The detonation was actually blowing up the spiritual building of demonic thoughts. This is what God had me do with the help of His amazing angels.

I asked the Lord after the explosion and subsequent cleaning took place, why the angels had to remove the spiritual elements of the stronghold. If it was torn down, why the need to remove it? His answer was poignant and made perfect sense. He said that if the debris remained (the evil thoughts and reasoning) the demonic would use the materials to begin rebuilding the stronghold. The angelic debris removal prevented the enemy from rebuilding strongholds with existing spiritual mindsets. My next trip to this same spot in D.C. revealed even more about this principle.

Time to Head Home

Once this was completed, I headed back to the airport and returned the car. Because of the delays earlier in the day, I missed my flight a second time and flew back on standby. I made it on the next plane and returned home safely.

I pray that as you read your excitement and desire to work with angels increases. There is no reason to fear. God said He only gives good gifts to His children. A trickle of truth can turn into a waterfall of truth as you walk with Jesus through this process. God has provided all the tools we need to be more than conquerors, and I firmly believe angels are a part of our weaponry.

The only thing we are allowed to fear in the Bible is the Lord. When we have a holy fear of God, this is a verse we can claim:

> *The angel of the Lord encamps around those who fear Him, and rescues them* (Psalm 34:7).

Take a few minutes to close your eyes and meditate on this. Having an awe and reverence for God invites God's angels to encircle you and give you great peace and rest. Remember, you are seeing the truth.

What About You?

- Do you feel you have a better understanding of what a demonic stronghold is?

- "As a man thinks in his heart, so is he" (Prov. 23:7 NKJV). How have you viewed the importance of your thoughts? After reading this chapter, has that perspective changed at all?

- Do you have any thoughts that do not line up with what God says in His Word? If so, spend a few minutes taking those thoughts captive in Jesus' name and renouncing the lies you have believed. Repent for believing them and ask the Holy Spirit to write His truth on your heart and in your mind. Memorize a scriptural promise to replace the wrong thought and thank God for His transforming power to experience the mind of Christ (see 1 Cor. 2:16).

Chapter 9

Washington, DC: Explosion in the Heavenlies Part II

by Joe Brock

The last chapter chronicled the trip I took to Washington, D.C. That trip was a significant step forward in understanding how to co-labor with angels to fulfill a commission God had given me. Since then, I have grown in both my view of the angelic and in interaction with angels in my daily Christian life.

Close to nine months had passed after this first trip to D.C. when I began having an almost daily vision of a large, grey, metal-alloy looking structure. It was in the shape of an upside-down boat. I could see the curvature on the sides of this thing where thick, heavy metal sheets were laid on top of each other with sizable, pronounced rivets binding them together. I could tell that it was not complete in construction; it was in the manufacturing stage.

117

The vision would appear in my mind for a second or two and would be gone just as quick. I have learned that when something like this happens, it is the Lord trying to show me something. When it first began occurring, it did not carry a lot of importance to me. As the months passed, I realized God was calling me to pray about this metal structure. It took no time for me to know precisely what God was showing me—the demonic was beginning to rebuild the stronghold I had destroyed, and this time it was not being built of bricks and mortar but an extremely powerful metal alloy.

Over the next three months, God methodically revealed to me what this structure was, why it was made of metal, and the significance of the metal. I knew I was going to be returning to D.C. Even months before my departure, I started seeing angels at the destination and knew they would be a significant part of this assignment.

When I say I already saw the angelic, I mean that each time my mind was drawn to this location, I could see a large number of angels in the spirit realm even though I was almost 600 physical miles away. Seeing in the spirit realm is not like seeing in the natural. There are things I can do in the spirit I cannot do in the physical, yet.

As I was watching the angels, I could see their assigned location began on the backside of the building on the sidewalk to the west. From here, they were spaced out a few feet apart and wrapped all the way around the building. I could clearly see over a hundred of them in preparation for a future time of ministry. I firmly believe that as we walk out our daily lives, the angelic is with us. There are times when God's purposes make them much more visible, and there are times that we will begin to see them around us as we quiet ourselves and focus.

We Struggle Not with Flesh and Blood

Over the next few months, God was preparing my heart for what was ahead. The metal structure I was seeing was a new stronghold the demonic was assembling at the exact spot I had destroyed the previous building. Where just a few months ago the fortress looked like brick and mortar, this time it was being built as an incredibly solid metal alloy. The Lord showed me the significance of this bulwark being metal.

For years I have prayed against strongholds in the U.S. and abroad. When you see areas with a singular, expansive evil permeating the region, we know this is a domain occupied by the demonic. I have learned to recognize strongholds by discerning the spiritual realm or identifying the sinful condition of people in the natural realm.

For this time of ministry in D.C., God was allowing me to see at least a part of what this spiritual fortress looked like in the heavens. When God revealed to me the difference between the brick and mortar building and the metal structure, I was utterly astounded.

A stronghold is a 'bulwark or fortress of thoughts.' A stronghold does not develop overnight; it is systematically erected over time. Thoughts that become solidified in the minds of society attract similar ideas. When you add them together, it's like adding a new room to a home. As this develops and grows, this mindset metastasizes into an actual ideology that seeks to control and influence the minds of the people it exercises authority over.

Just as a speaker produces sound waves that people within its range can hear, so too does a stronghold broadcast an evil that goes out over the minds of the people within its range. This broadcasted wickedness seeks to influence those who hear it to behave in a specific way.

For example, a fortress over San Francisco broadcasts homosexuality, and a stronghold over Las Vegas proclaims the desire to gamble. The goal of a stronghold is to control the people that live under it. If you spiritually study where you live, you can see what the strongholds are over your area. This is what Paul was referring to in 2 Corinthians:

> *Now I, Paul, myself urge you by the meekness and gentleness of Christ—I who am meek when face to face with you, but bold toward you when absent! I ask that when I am present I may not be bold with the confidence with which I propose to be courageous against some, who regard us as if we walked according to the flesh. For though we walk in the flesh, we do not war according to the flesh, for the weapons of our warfare are not of the flesh, **but divinely powerful for the destruction of fortresses. We are destroying speculations, and every lofty thing raised up against the knowledge of God, and we are taking every thought captive to the obedience of Christ,** and we are ready to punish all disobedience, whenever your obedience is complete* (2 Corinthians 10:1-6).

Spiritual fortresses seek to influence the way you think and believe, thereby drawing you into sin and rebellion. This is a stronghold, and this is what I was being sent back to D.C. to tear down once again.

Explanation

Let me explain the significance of the new metal building. When I was in college, a professor taught about the ten-year rule: that what is unimaginable today will be normal 10 years from now. Even in my lifetime I have seen this happen. Things that were deemed wrong and unthinkable are now the norm. Things I never saw in my youth are part of the daily lifestyle my children encounter. Thank God that where sin abounds grace abounds in greater measure, but it seems that society has become more tolerant to sin than ever before.

The federal building I had visited on my first trip to D.C. was of brick and mortar, which represented a spiritual stronghold that had existed since the mid-1800s. This is a long time for a specific prevailing thought to influence the U.S. The building was not modern, not up-to-date, and not as relevant as it had been at one time. This symbolized the slowing down of a particular evil mindset. The seeds planted a century ago had reached their maturity with not a lot of room for a demonic advancement.

When I pulled the stronghold down, I was pulling down mindsets that were becoming outdated. It was a great thing when this fortress fell. However, now the demonic was beginning to modernize evil mindsets. This is what the metal-alloy represented.

This is where the revelation became utterly fascinating to me. The Lord began to show me that the technological advancements over the last fifteen years or so have allowed the enemy to put evil before our eyes in a way that was not possible at any other time in the history of the world. In years past, it took weeks and in some cases months for information to travel. Now, with the internet, digital cameras, and smartphones, an event can be broadcast around the world within seconds of it happening or even *as* it is happening. We have witnessed more with our eyes and heard more with our ears than at any other time in history.

There is nothing intrinsically wrong with technology. The issue has never been technology; the problem has always been whose hand the technology has been placed in. I heard Ravi Zacharias tell the story of a conversation between D.L. Moody, the great American evangelist, and a young woman. He asked her how to rehabilitate a man with corrupt morals. Her answer was to send him to a university. Moody's response sums up the human condition: "If a man is stealing nuts and bolts from a railroad station and you send him to university, when his education is complete he will return and steal the whole railroad station." The problem is never with nuts and bolts; the issue is always the heart of man. Satan knows this all too well.

As technology has advanced, the human race has had more exposure to darkness than ever before. The Lord showed me that this has numbed and desensitized the human heart to the point that when we see something evil, we hardly give it a second thought. The enemy is using this as an opportunity to mold even the most stalwart Christian into someone who accepts darkness and does not question the effect it has on their life. The metal-alloy was symbolic of this. God showed me that the change from brick to this metal material represented the enemy's attempt to use higher levels of wickedness to construct strongholds that are more evil than previously seen in the United States.

The presence of darkness in all areas of technology empowers demons to build diabolical mindsets over cultures and societies. The evil around us seems to be growing at epidemic proportions, but the light inside of us is forever brighter than the dark around us. When we choose to arise and shine, the enemy's power cannot stand (see Isa. 61). This is why God calls us to pull down strongholds. In doing this, we remove the evil broadcasting around us and allow others to stop being influenced by the darkness. This is why I am sent to do the things I do.

When you consider the ramifications of a stronghold being built in an organization that has control over television, social media, the news, and significant parts of the government, it is no wonder God would want this destroyed. By tearing it down, the potential infiltration of evil into people's homes and lives is nullified, for at least a season, and allows the light of God's truth to go forth with less resistance.

Just as much as society itself grows and develops, so too does the desire of the demonic to use what is available to spread their evil mindsets. We must stop being naïve Christians who are blind to the diabolical agendas that surround us every day in all aspects of culture. We need better discernment.

Discernment is an easy thing to have; it is the result of beholding the Risen Christ. As you stare at Jesus and see Him in His multifaceted glory, whenever you look at something that does not resemble Him, you know the truth. Once you encounter Jesus, whatever does not remind you of Him is something to be handled with caution and wisdom.

Professor's Wisdom

One of my college professors was one of the most brilliant men I will ever meet. He could speak, read, and write in 20 languages. He had taught himself Latin to the point he could teach it at the seminary level. He was just as fluent in Biblical Hebrew as he was in Biblical Greek. He was academic through and through. He had a sensitive heart to the Holy Spirit and openly talked to me about the demonic and spiritual warfare. As we sat in his office, he brought up Romans 5:20:

> *Now the law came in to increase the trespass, but where sin increased, grace abounded all the more* (ESV).

I was surprised by what he then said: "Joe, if this verse is true, then as the darkness increases God's grace will increase all the more. Can you imagine what the people living during the tribulation time will be able to do? The Church will be able do things that rival anything we see in all of Scripture!"

It is one thing to hear a statement like this from someone without an advanced education. It is another thing entirely to listen to it from someone at his academic level. I saw that this man did not just study the

Bible, but he truly believed it. I think the things you are reading in this book are still in the adolescent stages of what God desires to do. How can we rightly place boundaries on the Holy Spirit?

It does not matter what your view is of the end times, one fact remains: the power and glory the Church will have at her disposal at the end of the age are exceeding, abundantly beyond anything any of our minds can conjure. What I am about to share about the tearing down of this stronghold is just the beginning of what God has for you and me.

The Journey Begins

Leading up to my second trip to D.C. God shared details of my mission to this federal building. He gave me specific instructions of things to do there and authorized me to bring a certain friend. God opened the heavens so anytime I even thought about the place, I could see angels stationed there waiting for our arrival. The Lord told me that these were not my personal angels, but angels He handpicked for this assignment. He said they were destruction angels sent there to assist me in the pulling down of this stronghold. I also sensed that this time there would be an implosion at the fortress rather than an explosion like I had seen on my last trip.

I knew I was to pour anointing oil on the ground again. I also knew we had to be cautious to not draw unwarranted attention to ourselves. The last thing the Lord instructed me to do was to read aloud Psalm 96 as we walked around the facility. When the time had come, my friend and I headed to Washington, D.C.

The plan was to drive all day and stay at a hotel very close to the ministry location. As we drove to D.C., I was praying about how to pour the anointing oil in a way to not to draw attention to ourselves. Very clearly in a vision, the Lord spoke to me and showed me a 20-ounce soda bottle.

He told to me to pour anointing oil into the bottle and carry it with us to our location. The color of the bottle was very close to the color of the oil so it would not draw unnecessary attention. Once we arrived, I was to take a pocket knife, poke a small hole in the bottom of the bottle and let it drip as we walked and prayed.

The Time Has Come

The next morning, shortly after waking, I began having visions of arrows with a very distinct look to them. The arrows' appearance had a sort of Celtic essence with dark steel and a raised, beveled head for the arrowhead. I was not sure what this meant but I shared it with my friend and we set out.

The plan was to arrive at the site and begin confessing and repenting right at 1:00 P.M. Due to the concern we could not find a parking spot, we arrived at the facility about forty-five minutes early. We parked about a half mile away and arrived with approximately twenty-five minutes to spare. To avoid looking too conspicuous, we slowly walked around the block the building was on and did our best to look like tourists.

As we approached the building, I could see the angels standing around as I had in the visions. They stood shoulder-to-shoulder all the way around the building like I had been shown. As 1:00 P.M. approached, we positioned ourselves at the starting point, I poked a hole in my soda bottle, and we began our walk around the building.

We started on the west side. We began walking slowly, praying in English and in tongues, and reading Psalm 96 from my cell phone. This was an excellent cover for us. If you look at any crowd nowadays, numerous heads are staring down at their phones. So as we walked, I stared at my phone and looked quite natural as I prayed and read Scriptures aloud.

The soda bottle streamed small inconspicuous drips of anointing oil as we walked, exactly as the Lord had shown me. As the oil dripped, I realized it was going to be used as a fuse. At that moment I was not sure how, but the answer came later that day. In the time leading up to the trip, the Lord showed me in a vision that foot activity would be abundant immediately in front of the building on the day and time we were to pray. I saw numerous men and women exiting and entering the facility. As we turned the corner while walking and praying, I could see ahead of me an immediate increase in foot traffic around the entrance of the building. This was precisely what I had seen in the vision and felt like a precious confirmation to me.

We continued walking in front of the building through the path of angels who had been standing there for months. Something unexpected then happened. In the spirit realm, an immense group of angels surrounded me in an oval pattern. They were standing with their backs to me facing outward and each angel was holding a large drawn bow and arrow. Because I had been staring at the phone, I was able to stop in front of the facility to take all this in.

I felt very safe and secure at that moment. After a minute or so of absorbing this all, we then walked to the end of the building where some employees were outside having their lunch. As we moved past them, I stopped and looked back, seeking the Lord to see if there was anything left to do. The Lord told me I would blow up the stronghold later that day.

As we transitioned past the building, we came to the home immediately adjacent to the facility where we had just prayed. There was a metal fence along the sidewalk surrounding this house. As we approached it, I was in shock—the fence was made up of thin, square, connected bars with an arrowhead on the top! The arrowhead was the *exact* type I had seen earlier in the day in a vision!

I was stunned.

The Lord usually confirms things at the end of a trip like this. On this assignment, He kindly gave confirmations systemically as the day progressed. We didn't question or doubt we were in God's will. We knew that all we saw in the spirit was authentic and legitimate. We returned to our vehicle and left to find something for lunch.

Detonation and Falling Words

After touring D.C. for a short time, we ended up stopping at a fantastic place called The District Wharf. It is a large boardwalk area on the Potomac River where boats can dock and are aligned with shops, stores, and restaurants. We parked in a garage and entered the facility.

My travel companion and I briefly got separated. It was during this time of separation that the Lord told me it was time to set off the detonator. I found an isolated and secluded place (in the most glorious bathroom stall I have ever seen!) and was immediately taken into a vision.

The Lord showed me the place we had been, He once again showed me the angels, and lastly, He showed me that the oil I had dripped onto the ground had become a spiritual fuse line. Each drip of the oil would itself explode and would then be the catalyst to detonate the next drop. When I set off the detonator, the first drop of oil on the west side of the building would explode and the next one and so on. The anointing oil had been spread around the entire perimeter of the building and proved to be an impressive sight.

Staying in the vision, I was given the same type of detonation device I had used on the first trip. I readied myself, then pulled up on the plunger and pushed it down. From where I was positioned in the vision, I saw the explosions on the side of the building that then moved along the path of oil across the entire front. I saw every single blast, one after another.

The fascinating thing to me was that as the oil exploded, sidewalk portions (in the spirit realm) were blowing up. One sidewalk segment after the other was exploding right before my spiritual eyes. As the sidewalk exploded, bare soil was left in its place in the outline of the sidewalk section. As the section was cleared and the dirt remained, a garden immediately began growing out of the ground with scores of small, beautiful flowers. By the time the last oil drop exploded and the area was replaced with flowers, the entire facility was surrounded by a gorgeous flower garden planted directly by the hand of God.

As the sidewalks were being detonated, there was another, even more significant implosion. The metal-alloy looking demonic stronghold imploded into itself.

What happened next was the most amazing, life-defining moment of the trip. When the stronghold imploded, the debris that was falling was not metal or rock or any physically perceived substance. What was falling all around...*were words and sentences.* Scattered all over the ground were sentences lying on and piling over themselves. I was overwhelmed.

Please bear in mind that I had found a quiet place to pray in a granite-floored bathroom stall. I could hardly contain myself. I saw sentences, hundreds and hundreds of sentences. If you could hold a piece of paper in front of you that was covered in sentences, and the words of the sentences were able to slide off the sheet and pile up on the floor, that is what it looked like.

As I looked more intently at the words in the piles, I saw some words in bold print. I also saw some words highlighted and some underlined. Some words were in different colors, and I even saw one word highlighted like it would be if you hovered your computer mouse over it. It looked like something was to be done to this particular word, but the implosion happened before this could take place. It was something I will never, ever forget.

An Angel and a Vacuum Cleaner

Having been in the warfare and inner healing ministries of the Holy Spirit, the significance of this event resonated deeply inside me. I mentioned earlier that strongholds are demonically established systems of thoughts. Demons strive to convince us of lies. As we heed them and are deceived by them, the lies become evil spiritual structures both inside and outside us.

What I correctly saw was what the stronghold was—words on a page. I saw demons taking their plans to develop a more profound and sinister evil by putting them on paper. When the power of Christ and His cross engaged this stronghold, Truth overwhelmingly triumphed, and demonic lies were destroyed. The enemy's attempt to establish a new, more advanced darkness was thwarted by obedience to the Lord's commands. Then another angel appeared.

As I stayed in the bathroom stall and watched this staggering display unfold in front of me, a very, very large angel came into the vision. This was somewhat comical to me. This large angel appeared in the vision carrying a vacuum cleaner that was proportionally sized to it. The angel was higher up, elevated above the other elements of the vision.

The vacuum he held was a standard upright model, red, with a single handle, a fabric bag that hung off the handle, and a cleaning apparatus at the bottom. The Lord showed me this was a commercial vacuum utilized for bigger jobs. The angel was using what was necessary to get the job done.

As the vision played out, I watched the angel begin vacuuming up all these demonic sentences off the floor. When there were no more words, the angel then detached the bag from the back of the vacuum and handed it to me. As I reached out to take the bag, I knew that only Jesus could totally destroy the contents. Even if I burned it, the demons would try to use the ashes to rebuild the stronghold. I did not know why the angel gave it to me.

Then, all of a sudden an opening appeared in front of me. It resembled a furnace chute you would see in an older building. I knew the angel wanted me to drop this bag down the shaft. I looked down the chute and saw a red glow deep, deep down. The Lord then spoke to me inside the vision, "Send it back to hell because that is where it came from." I knew that it would be so utterly destroyed in hell that not even ashes would remain. I dropped it down the chute and, at that moment, the vision and our mission were complete.

I caught back up with my friend; we had lunch and went back to the hotel for a spiritual debriefing. The exciting thing about this trip is that with the ongoing confirmations, there was no need to debrief in as much detail as I had done in trips past. We headed out the next morning and arrived safely home.

Let the Awakening Begin

Between what Charity and I have shared, I truly hope you are beginning to awaken to all the potential God has bound up in you. You are alive in Christ, you carry the nature of Jesus, and you have everyday angels with you, waiting for your directions.

God may not send you to the nation's capital to partner with angels, but He may send you downtown to your local courthouse. Or to your child's middle school, or across the street to your neighbor's house. It is not about where He sends us; it is about our obedience to the assignment.

Being called to a local church or neighborhood or being called across the world is not the issue. Wherever you are called is the most important place in the world for you to be, and you have angels there to assist you.

The book of James says we have not because we ask not. If we flip this around though, we can say then that we have because we ask. Ask your Father to teach you about your angels and how they are to be involved in your purpose. It is very exciting. Pray this prayer with me:

> *Father, thank You for the angels You have sent to minister to me. If I have not honored them in my life, I repent. I see in Scripture it is Your design to include angels in Your Kingdom, and it is my desire to partner with You and them in advancing Your Kingdom on the earth. I pray that the eyes of my heart would be enlightened to see in the spirit all that You have to show me, and I purpose to honor what You reveal. Thank You, Father, for Your perfect plans and that the life You designed me to live is supernatural and spiritual, filled with spiritual beings. I'm excited and expectant for all You will continue to show me about Your holy angels. In Jesus' name I pray, Amen.*

What About You?

☐ Throughout the book, I talk about going to certain geographic areas to do warfare because where there is war, there is an enemy. Has God ever sent you to a specific place for a supernatural assignment? Where did you go and what was your experience?

☐ How have you tended to view the importance of your words? After reading this chapter, has that perspective changed at all?

☐ Read Proverbs 18:21, Matthew 12:37, and Psalm 141:3. What do these Scriptures reveal about the power of your words?

☐ If necessary, repent for any idle words you have spoken and purpose by God's grace to express only His life-giving words of truth from now on (see Eph. 4:29).

Chapter 10

Angelic Interaction: Dangerous or Divine?

by Charity Kayembe

One of my favorite comments from a blog reader was: "These angel posts are priceless. They make heavenly encounters more about lifestyle, and make the Kingdom of God habitational rather than visitational..."

I love the idea that it doesn't have to be "encounters" or "visitations" where angels come and go. They are always with us! We can always take the initiative to step into this realm and live to this Kingdom reality anytime we choose.

Take It or Not

But I wondered, is that right? Are we really supposed to be taking initiative? Jesus said He did nothing on His own initiative, but only what He saw Father doing (see John 5:19-20). Obviously, we want to be like Jesus, so we shouldn't be taking the initiative (see John 5:30).

However, Scripture encourages us over and over to be proactive in our walk in the spirit: set your mind on the spirit (see Rom 8:5), keep seeking the things above (see Col. 3:1-3), look at the things that are unseen (see 2 Cor. 4:18). The Bible makes it clear we should take the initiative to live by the Spirit.

Then God showed me that it's not one or the other, but both. Jesus could only relinquish His initiative after He had taken the initiative to step into the spirit realm.

Because if we don't take the initiative and step into the supernatural realm, meet Jesus and His angels, and find out what they are up to, we are forced to take the initiative with every other thing we do and say. If we live outside of the spirit, we make decisions based only on what we can see and hear in the natural world.

However, if we simply choose to take the initiative to step into the sacred supernatural, to look for vision, to listen to Heaven—take the initiative to live into the spirit realm, that's it! That's the only initiative we need to take. We are then positioned to see what Father's doing and hear what angels are saying, so we can work together with them and live like Jesus, who was only moved by what He perceived in the supernatural realm.

What Not to Do

We are often much too passive in our walk in the spirit. We put it all on God and say, "Well, if He wants me to see or hear an angel then He should just knock me off my feet with a blinding light like Saul. That's the way He did it in the Bible!"

While God can do that, that is obviously not His preferred method of communication. God can also make a donkey talk to you, but these scriptural examples are not anything we want to emulate. More than anything, they are examples showing us what not to do.

Does God need to blind us for three days in order for us to hear His message? If I am a prophet, and my donkey has more spiritual discernment than I do, I think I need to reconsider my vocation.

It pleases God when we take the initiative to interact with Him and the angelic partners He created for us. We are to seek first His Kingdom, and it is a heavenly Kingdom, filled with heavenly angels (see Matt. 6:33).

How do we seek that Kingdom? By taking initiative to step into the supernatural world and actively look for vision, rather than waiting around for a blinding light to knock us to the ground. By actively initiating a conversation with angels rather than waiting around for our donkey to tell us about the angelic vision he's seeing in the spirit (see Num. 22:21-35).

Angel Talk

Anyone who has seen a Christmas pageant knows that angels talk with people: Hark, the herald angels sing, glory to the newborn King! When the shepherds heard the angels, they didn't worry if they were being deceived and doubt the revelation. Instead, they acted in faith believing the message was from God: "Let us go straight to Bethlehem then, and see this thing that has happened which the Lord has made known to us" (see Luke 2:8-15). The shepherds took the message from the angel as a message from God Himself, and as a result of their obedience to what the angel said, they were the first ones to meet Jesus (see Luke 2:16-20).

Throughout Scripture, angels often brought messages from God to people. In fact, the literal meaning of the word "angel" in both Hebrew and Greek is "messenger." So clearly, angels speak to us, for that is their very name and function. That is what messengers do—they give messages.

Apostolic pastor Dr. Tim Sheets thoroughly unpacks this revelation from the original biblical languages in his book *Angel Armies*. He explains that once we understand the meaning of the word "angel," it should not be at all surprising that they bring us messages.

> There are many today in the body of Christ who freely say what the devil has been telling them, but if you say what the angels have been telling you, they think that's weird. This must stop. We must embrace angel assistance. Let's be clear—listening to demons is weird. Listening to angels is normal Christianity.[9]

Who Do You Think You Are?

While we now understand that angels can talk to us, are we allowed to speak with them? What kind of authority do we have and how does God see us? In Psalm 8:3-6, David asks this very question and reveals the extraordinary answer:

> *When I consider Your heavens, the work of Your fingers, the moon and the stars, which You have ordained; what is man that You take thought of him, and the son of man that You care for him? Yet You have made him a little lower than God, and You crown him with glory and majesty! You make him to rule over the works of Your hands; You have put all things under his feet.*

We are just "a little lower than God!" While some versions render the translation "a little lower than angels," the Hebrew word in the verse is *Elohim*, which always refers to God Himself.

We have been crowned with majesty and made to rule. Over what? Over everything. "The works of His hands" could not be more inclusive and unquestionably includes angels. This is even reiterated in the next phrase, "You have put all things under" our feet.

This revelation of our identity is confirmed throughout Scripture. We are the only ones made in God's image, and as believers, we are not only His family, but also His Body (see 1 Cor. 12:27). Our spirit has been joined with Holy Spirit (see 1 Cor. 6:17). We are seated with Christ in heavenly places (see Eph. 2:6). We are partakers of the divine nature, and we have been filled with the fullness of God (see 2 Pet. 1:4; Eph. 3:19).

Little "g" gods

In fact, there is another amazing passage in Psalms that speaks to our true identity as well. Psalm 82:6 declares, "You are gods, and all of you are sons of the Most High." Really? While we don't usually think of ourselves in this way, it actually dovetails seamlessly with the Genesis account of our beginning.

We know we have been created in the image of God (see Gen. 1:27). Scripture also makes clear that everything reproduces after its own kind (see Gen. 1:21-25). That is, the children of birds are little birds and the children of zebras are little zebras. It follows naturally then that the children of God would be little gods. We are certainly not God Himself, but we are absolutely children made in His divine likeness with His own DNA. We are little copies of Him (see 1 John 3:9). He breathed into us His very breath; His Spirit flows through us and gives us life (see Gen. 2:7).

Just in case we are tempted to relegate this revelation to some obscure passages in the Old Testament, Jesus actually highlights it for us in the Gospels to be sure we don't miss it.

Jesus answered them, "Has it not been written in your Law, 'I said, you are gods'?" (John 10:34).

Jesus even went on to say that this truth is the word of God and Scripture cannot be broken (see John 10:35). Indeed, we are the supernatural progeny of God Himself (see 1 Pet. 1:23).

Once we understand who we are, it will be natural for us to speak with angels. We know that angels are ministering spirits sent to render service to us who inherit salvation (see Heb. 1:14). They are here to serve us, and Paul even says that we are going to judge them (see 1 Cor. 6:3). What does that say about the authority God has entrusted to us?

Delegated Authority

My dad, Mark Virkler, shares the story of how he learned it was right to commission angels.

> When I first looked and saw my guardian angel, I saw a 10-foot warrior angel, dressed with armor and a shield and a sword. He was standing at attention and motionless at my side. After seeing this for several days and feeling perplexed, I asked myself, "Does he think the war is over? I'm sure still fighting." So since I couldn't figure it out, I went to the Lord in two-way journaling and asked Him why my warrior angel was doing nothing.
>
> Jesus answered, "Because you have never commissioned him." I said, "Well, I thought angels were under Your authority, not mine."

His response was, "Yes, they are under My authority, but I have seated you with Me to rule and reign (see Eph. 2:6; Gen. 1:28), and part of your training for rulership is to commission your angel. As long as you are under My authority, your guardian angel will be under your authority (see Ps. 8:6). If you ever step out from under My authority, then your guardian angel will no longer be under your authority. Commission him to fight. He will go, he will fight, and he will win."

So I began commissioning my warrior angel, and sure enough, I would see him go, flash his sword a couple of times, win, and return within seconds.

Heir Force

Dr. Sheets teaches extensively on commissioning angels because of a dramatic encounter he had with the Lord.

One day, I again drove out to the lake to pray and to think about the angel network and the strategies needed to overcome narcissism in the church. As I was pulling alongside the lake, the Holy Spirit spoke another word to me. This word was very forceful and bold. Although very rare for me, He spoke this word audibly and so loudly that I had to pull the car over to the side and stop. I was shaking.

The words were like a command as He boldly said, "Release My Heir Force," meaning the force behind the heirs. I knew immediately He meant "heir" and not "air." That word became an apostolic assignment that I have since carried everywhere I've gone.[10]

Scripture explains that angels obey the word of the Lord and it is their delight to do His will (see Ps. 103:20-21). They listen when we speak God's Word and pray scriptural promises. When God speaks in our hearts what He wants done, and we give voice to that, angels listen and are moved to action, too. Gabriel told Daniel, "I have come because of your words" (see Dan. 10:12). By coming into agreement with God and His word, we are activating the standing orders that angels have, so they are immediately released to accomplish Father's plan.

The Angel's Sword

Csaba and Eva Gegeny are an anointed couple leading Dunamis Ministries in Hungary. They coordinated our workshop on dream interpretation in Budapest, and we enjoyed swapping stories of supernatural adventures. One of the visions Eva shared powerfully illustrates what is going on in the spirit world when we pray.

She saw a huge warrior angel standing at attention. He didn't move until she prayed. When she began speaking, the words that came out of her mouth were a sword. Because of her prayers, the angel had something to hold onto. He took the sword and was now ready to fight as her words had both equipped and released him for battle. Indeed, the sword of the Spirit is the word of God (see Eph. 6:17).

If we are ever unsure what to say or how to release our angels, we can allow Holy Spirit to help us by speaking in tongues (see Rom. 8:26-27). The Spirit will intercede through us for the saints according to the will of God, and angels have no problem translating this prayer language!

We see then how Father invites us to work together with Him through delegated authority. He calls angels to minister to us and He calls us to commission angels. It is a team effort where His children co-labor with His angels. Pastor Bill Johnson writes,

On numerous occasions throughout Scripture angels did what God could have done easily Himself. But why didn't God do those things Himself? For the same reason He doesn't preach the gospel: He has chosen to let His creation enjoy the privilege of service in His Kingdom.[11]

Indeed, it is our honor to partner with God in advancing His Kingdom on the earth, and one strategic way we do this is by partnering with angels.

Gabriel and Daniel

As we have mentioned, most of us are already talking with angels and don't even realize it. We are familiar with the biblical commands to resist the devil or rebuke and bind the enemy. Usually we resist and rebuke him by speaking to him, and satan is a fallen angel. So, we are already engaging the angelic.

As revivalist Dr. David Herzog confirms,

> What's interesting to me is that pastors and Christians can tell me all about the demons over their cities. They have maps and grids and can point to the streets where the demons are. But when I ask, "What are the territorial angels over your city?" they can't name even one... Most people know about territorial spirits, but they know about the demonic not the angelic. If you bring the angel who is supposed to be ruling that city and unleash him, things will happen![12]

But are we really allowed to have conversations with angels? Is it okay for us to actually communicate back and forth? Yes, conversations with angels are not only spiritual, but entirely scriptural. Daniel said,

"Gabriel whom I had seen in the vision came... and talked with me" (see Dan. 9:21-22).

There are entire chapters of the Bible devoted to recording such angelic interaction, for example, in the books of Zechariah and Daniel (see Zech. 1:7–6:15; Dan. 7:15-28; 8:13-27; 9:20–10:21). In the New Testament there are back and forth conversations between angels and people as well.

In the first chapter of the Gospel of Luke, the angel Gabriel told Mary she was going to have a baby. She didn't understand how that could be, since she was a virgin, so she asked him about it. (Notice Mary did not ask God; she asked the angel.) Gabriel answered her question explaining that Holy Spirit was going to do a supernatural miracle. Mary believed the angel and spoke with him again, expressing her faith in what he had told her. She trusted the angel was from God and acted on his message (see Luke 1:26-38).

Another scriptural example of a back-and-forth conversation with an angel is recorded in the book of Revelation. John went to an angel and told him to give him a little book. The angel said, "Okay, you can have it, but you won't like it." The angel gave him the book, and John agreed he didn't like it (see Rev. 10:9-10).

It's important to notice what happened right before this angelic conversation. In verse eight, we find that it was actually God who told John to go to the angel and get the book (see Rev. 10:8). So yes, we can tell angels to do things, but we are still led by the Lord in these interactions, just as we are led by Him in all our relationships and conversations. We live and walk by the Spirit (see Gal. 5:25)!

Matthew 16:18-19 speaks to this understanding of divine initiative and I appreciate how the Amplified Bible Classic Edition brings out the original meaning of the Greek:

I will build My church, and the gates of Hades (the powers of the infernal region) *shall not overpower it [or be strong to its detriment or hold out against it]. I will give you the keys of the kingdom of heaven; and whatever you bind* (declare to be improper and unlawful) *on earth must be what is already bound in Heaven; and whatever you loose* (declare lawful) *on earth must be what is already loosed in Heaven.*

We look into the spirit to see what Jesus is up to and what Father has planned, and then we agree with that. We're not just making things up as we go along; we are modeling the example of Heaven. "Your kingdom come, Your will be done, on earth as it is in heaven" (Matt. 6:10). Sickness and sin are bound—declared unlawful and not allowed—in Heaven, so we bind them here. Angels and holiness are loosed—released and allowed to move freely—in Heaven, so we loose them here. And often the easiest way to loose angels is by talking with them.

Unemployment Line

Unfortunately, Joe has seen multitudes of angels restlessly milling about, not doing anything at all. When he inquired of the Lord, He explained there's a bit of an "unemployment line" for angels in the heavenlies, as most of His kids aren't giving them any work to do.

Many other leaders in the Body of Christ have testified to seeing the same. In his book *Heaven's Host*, prophetic minister Bobby Connor writes,

> Once my eyes were opened and I could see into the heavens, where I saw untold thousands of angels. They appeared to be bored, so I asked, "Lord, why are they bored?"

"Because the saints of God have not activated them into action," He said.[13]

In his book *Secrets of the Seer*, Jamie Galloway, shares a similar experience:

> I kept seeing angels that were sitting around not doing anything. I did not know what to make of this, and I began to wonder if certain angels were just lazy! It kept happening—when I saw them, they looked bored, like they were in need of something to do!
>
> I asked the Holy Spirit, and He spoke to my heart: "These are unemployed angels. They are waiting for a job." I responded, "Are You going to give them one?" He spoke back: "I have given My children stewardship over My works on the earth..."[14]

Bored, lazy and restless are not words we want describing our heavenly armies! This is why we must partner with them and with God by activating their marching orders and releasing them to accomplish His assignments for them. Again, often the easiest way to release them is by talking with them.

While talking definitely leads to conversation, there is something our conversations with angels doesn't lead to. Worshiping angels is something we never do and is what we will examine next.

Angel of Light?

The biggest concern some Christians have regarding angelic interaction is that they fear satan will come as an angel of light and they will accidentally start worshiping him. The good news is, *there is no record in Scripture of any believer actually doing that*. It is also significant that the clearest instruction we have on not worshiping angels was delivered by an angel himself!

That is a huge revelation in itself, and we are going to look carefully at those accounts of John, who mistakenly tried to worship a holy angel. First, let's examine the verse about the angel of light, since that has also been greatly misunderstood.

What do those verses in Second Corinthians actually say? What is the context?

> *For such men are false apostles, deceitful workers, disguising themselves as apostles of Christ. No wonder, for even satan disguises himself as an angel of light. Therefore it is not surprising if his servants also disguise themselves as servants of righteousness, whose end will be according to their deeds.* (2 Corinthians 11:13-15)

We can start by understanding what Paul is not saying. He is not discussing worship. The focus of his conversation is not satan. Paul is writing about false apostles who pretend to be good but they are not. That is what this passage is about.

Then, almost off-handedly, he mentions satan. You could paraphrase the verse this way:

> False apostles pretending to be apostles of Christ? No wonder; even satan tries to make himself out to be an angel of light. It's not a surprise his followers do the same! But no matter, they will all be exposed.

We recognize immediately that, more than anything, this is simply a discussion about deceptive people in the Corinthian church. Just because there are false apostles or false prophets, does that mean we reject all apostles and prophets? Surely not, since Paul was an apostle himself. So too, just because there are fallen angels doesn't mean we systematically reject all angels.

Of course, we want to glean any secrets Paul may be revealing about our enemy in this passage, but have we potentially misinterpreted his words? Obviously, unbelievers who don't have the Spirit of Christ in them can and will be deceived by satan. They are already deceived by him. Their hearts have been blinded and they live in spiritual darkness.

Paul says that before we were saved we were darkness (see Eph. 5:8). This is how satan can disguise himself and appear as an angel of light to unbelievers.

But that has nothing to do with you.

As Christians, we are no longer in the darkness (see 1 Thess. 5:4). We are children of light and children of the day; we do not belong to the night or to the darkness (see 1 Thess. 5:5). We walk in the light as He is in the light (see 1 John 1:7). Jesus, the Light of the World, is alive in us and now we are light in the Lord (see Eph. 5:8)!

Our eyes have been opened: Truth is a Person and He lives in us (see John 14:6). His Spirit of Truth enlightens us and His discernment guides us into all truth (see John 16:13). First John 2:20 tells us that we have His anointing to know truth and the passage goes on to say,

> *I have written these things to you about those who are trying to deceive you. And as for you, the anointing you received from Him remains in you, and you do not need anyone to teach you. But just as His true and genuine anointing teaches you about all things, so remain in Him as you have been taught.* (1 John 2:26-27 BSB)

Therefore, we do not need to be afraid since God Himself is teaching us and leading us. We can be confident that any "light" the enemy may use to attempt to disguise himself pales in comparison to the Shekinah glory of God that dwells within us and radiates through us.

In the next chapter, we are going to carefully examine biblical parameters for spirit realm navigation. These requirements are absolutely essential to safely step into the sacred supernatural. For now, let's simply understand that when Paul mentioned satan masquerading as an angel of light, he was not somehow trying to subtly warn the Corinthian Christians about the angelic realm. Surely if the Lord had intended to caution us about angelic interaction He could have been more straightforward about it.

After all, God knows how to lay down the law. Throughout Scripture we have no trouble finding direct and clear commands of what to do and what not to do. It is remarkable that nowhere in the Bible does Father ever specifically warn His precious children of the "perilous risks" of angelic interaction. Doesn't He love us? Doesn't He care?

Or, is it that angelic interaction is not as dangerous as we have made it out to be?

Worshiping Angels

As we have mentioned, there are literally hundreds of pro-angel verses in the Bible: They protect us, they partner with us in evangelism, they bring us messages from God. Then we have two verses (the one we just looked at and one more) that seem to say something negative, and all of a sudden we're tempted to dismiss angels entirely and let fear steal away God's blessings from us.

If we look at the Law of Proportion, we are comparing 2 Scriptures with 300. We must take all of the Bible into consideration in order to get the whole counsel of God on the matter. We would never want to let those two verses nullify the other three hundred.

However, that is essentially what we do if we let doubt and fear creep into our hearts and we tell God, "I'm too scared to talk with angels because I might somehow end up worshiping them."

What? That is such a huge jump. We are talking about having conversations with angels and co-laboring together with angels, but nobody said anything about wanting to worship them. Let's take a look at the one other passage that seems to confuse people so much.

> *Therefore no one is to act as your judge in regard to food or drink or in respect to a festival or a new moon or a Sabbath day—things which are a mere shadow of what is to come; but the substance belongs to Christ. Let no one keep defrauding you of your prize by delighting in self-abasement and the worship of the angels, taking his stand on visions he has seen, inflated without cause by his fleshly mind, and not holding fast to the head, from whom the entire body, being supplied and held together by the joints and ligaments, grows with a growth which is from God.* (Colossians 2:16-19)

So that's it. That's the big verse that as soon as you consider talking with your angels, satan is going to remind you of. I have seen people shy away from talking with angels just to be on the safe side. They reason that it's better to not talk with them, because you might start worshiping them.

Letting the Enemy Win

Pastor Bill Johnson says that fear often masquerades as wisdom. Professing to be wise, they became fools (see Rom. 1:22). Satan knows that if he can get us scared of being deceived, so that we decide it is better to not engage the angelic at all, then he's already won.

He just ate our lunch. Because while we may not have been deceived and bowed down to an angel in a vision, we just let the fallen angel satan deceive us with his words. And when we agree with his lies, we are essentially bowing down to him and his suggestions in our hearts. Worship, more than anything else, is a matter of the heart.

If we are in fear, he's won. If we are afraid that we're going to be deceived, satan has already accomplished his goal, because now we are not even going to try to have an angelic conversation or interact with the supernatural. The enemy wins by default, because we don't even show up.

If the devil can't get us to do something bad, then he will just try to keep us from doing something good. Do you see how sneaky that is? Do you see why we don't ever want to be afraid? Fear is faith in satan and believing he has more power to get us than God has power to protect us.

Slaves Through Fear

Because the truth is, the enemy has already lost. He is thoroughly defeated. The only way he can win is if we re-empower him through our belief in his lies and our agreement with them. It is we who empower him through our fear. Otherwise, he's got nothing on us.

The Bible says we were slaves through fear, but God delivered us when He rendered the devil powerless. As in, no power (see Heb. 2:14-15). We know that greater is Jesus in us than anyone in the world (see 1 John 4:4). We know that we are more than conquerors through Him who loves us (see Rom. 8:37). We know that God always leads us in triumph in Christ (see 2 Cor. 2:14).

So, all we need to do is resist the devil, and he flees (see James 4:7). We rebuke him, and he's gone (see Luke 4:35). It doesn't have to be a long, drawn-out struggle. The war is over. All we need to do now is stand firm in the already won victory of Christ (see Eph. 6:11-14).

What the Verse Is Not Saying

What are those verses in Colossians talking about then? They specifically address listening to someone else who thinks they are spiritual because of their visions or because they worship angels. They are just telling us not to pay attention to someone who worships angels.

More importantly, let's look at what the passage is not saying. It is not saying: "Colossian Christians, don't worship your angels." Because our holy guardian angels will never receive our worship. They are faithful to God, so that is essentially a nonissue.

Instead, this passage is referring to some prideful, judgmental person with vain ramblings. This person is not holding fast to the head, who is Jesus, which means he's not even a Christian. And this unbeliever worships angels. Well yes, obviously, they shouldn't do that, but there are a lot of other things they're doing that they shouldn't be doing either.

We don't care what this person is saying. We don't care what this person is doing. In fact, that is what Paul is telling them: "Don't let him judge you. Don't even listen to him."

That's it.

It is not a stern and frightening warning to Christians about having conversations with the guardian angels Father assigned to us. It is not a cautionary threat about engaging or partnering with our holy angels. This is significant. It is important for us to always look at Scriptures in context to gain a clear understanding of God's heart.

Scary Warning or Promised Blessing

In fact, worst case scenario, what happens if we do accidentally get confused somehow and bow down before our angel? Is there hellfire and brimstone? Fury and judgment? Or, at the very least, divine disappointment over our mistake?

None of the above. Nobody gets upset at all actually.

There are two Scriptures in the book of Revelation that I have heard used as severe warnings or threats: "Better not worship angels. Naughty, shame on you." Let's examine both verses and see what they actually say.

> *Then I fell at his feet to worship him. But he said to me, "Do not do that; I am a fellow servant of yours and your brethren who hold the testimony of Jesus; worship God. For the testimony of Jesus is the spirit of prophecy."* (Revelation 19:10)

> *I, John, am the one who heard and saw these things. And when I heard and saw, I fell down to worship at the feet of the angel who showed me these things. But he said to me, "Do not do that. I am a fellow servant of yours and of your brethren the prophets and of those who heed the words of this book. Worship God."* (Revelation 22:8-9)

I want to re-frame these Scriptures for you so that you see how they are actually wonderful promises from your loving heavenly Father. They are blessings! They are a huge confirmation and example to us that we have absolutely nothing to worry about.

What Doesn't Happen

How can we be so sure? Because every time a believer bowed down to worship an angel in Scripture, the angel said, "Oh hey, wait a sec.

Actually, it's just me, your fellow servant! Let's go worship God together." And the vision continues. No punishment is given. No condemnation or wrath meted out. There's not even a guilt trip.

Imagine the scene: John falls at the feet of an angel to worship him. Jesus is right there and sees the whole thing! Does He get upset? Is He angry? What about sad? Is Jesus offended? Did John hurt His feelings? Not at all.

It is almost like Jesus is laughing and saying, "My bad! It was ME who sent My angel to you, sorry for the mix up!" Obviously, He doesn't use those exact words, but it's pretty close (see Rev. 22:16).

So instead of incurring dreadful consequences, or, at the very least a harsh reprimand, what happens?

Nothing happens.

The angel *continues* sharing heavenly secrets with John (see Rev. 22:10-11). Jesus *continues* telling him wonderful revelations and promises (see Rev. 22:12ff). There are no negative repercussions whatsoever.

We must feel God's heart on this. "Don't be afraid, little ones, for it is your Father's good pleasure to give you the kingdom" (Luke 12:32). Once we understand His perspective, we will never be afraid of "accidentally worshiping" angels again.

What Does Jesus Think?

When asked about prayer, Jesus said:

Or what man is there among you who, when his son asks for a loaf, will give him a stone? Or if he asks for a fish, he will not give him a snake, will he? If you then, being evil, know how to give good gifts to your children, how much more will your Father who is in heaven give what is good to those who ask Him! (Matthew 7:9-11)

If we go into our quiet times with the Lord asking for an angelic encounter, is He going to give us a demonic counterfeit? Do we believe He's a good Dad who can keep us out of trouble and protected? Do we think His power to keep us is greater than the enemy's power to reach us?

If we believe God is going to keep us safe and sound for all eternity in the spiritual realm of Heaven, then we can probably also trust Him enough to keep us safe and sound in the spiritual realm now while we chat with some angels for a few minutes.

The Only Way to Please God

Faith is the currency of Heaven (see Heb. 11:6). It is what we can give to a God who has everything: our faith, our trust, our strong belief in His strong love. If we are in fear, we are questioning either His goodness or His sovereignty. We purpose to know and believe the love God has for us, because that is what casts out the fear (see 1 John 4:16-18).

Father has gotten us this far, how could we worry that He's going to let us down now? He doesn't know how to fail, and we cannot trust Him too much. Indeed, Jesus told us that the work of God is to believe (see John 6:29)!

Now that we have firmly established that we are not worshiping angels and can live without fearing that we will accidentally do so, it is time to move on to the practical "how-to's" for stepping into the spirit. In the next chapter, we will explore biblical safeguards for our journey and examine some foundational keys to help you begin to engage the supernatural. It's time to unlock the Kingdom of God within you!

What About You?

- Had you heard there was an angelic "unemployment line" in Heaven? What do you think will happen on earth once those warriors receive their marching orders?

- Have you ever commissioned an angel for an assignment? What happened?

- Prayerfully meditate on Psalm 8:3-6 and ask Holy Spirit to give you a heart revelation of your identity as a son or daughter of God.

  When I consider Your heavens, the work of Your fingers,
  The moon and the stars, which You have ordained;
  What is man that You take thought of him,
  And the son of man that You care for him?
  Yet You have made him a little lower than God,
  And You crown him with glory and majesty!
  You make him to rule over the works of Your hands;
  You have put all things under his feet.

- What does this passage mean to you personally? What might this truth look like exemplified in your life?

- Have you been taught that you can't interact with angels? Have you been afraid of getting to know them because of this?

- If so, take some time in prayer to forgive those who put that seed of fear in your heart and confess your fears to the Lord. Repent for believing any lie about angels that was contrary to the Word of God. Ask Holy Spirit to renew your mind to His perspective on angels and release His faith in you. Let God's love drive out the fear and replace it with His Kingdom emotions of hope and excited expectation for all He wants to do in your life through the ministry of His angels.

Chapter 11

The Sacred Supernatural: Rules for Engagement

by Charity Kayembe

Now that we understand the Bible not only gives us permission to interact with angels, but encouragement to do so, the big question becomes: how do we do that?

Let's start with the short answer: Simply have a conversation with Jesus and ask Him to make some angelic introductions! Angels are spirits and God is Spirit, so we connect with these spiritual beings in the spirit realm the same way we connect with Jesus.

In my parent's revelatory training on the *4 Keys to Hearing God's Voice*, they teach that "Hearing God's voice is as simple as: quieting yourself down, looking for vision, tuning to spontaneity, and writing."[15] It is easy enough for a child to do and my dad has traveled around the world for 40 years bringing hundreds of thousands of believers into daily conversational relationship with their heavenly Father.

In the back of this book, there is an appendix they wrote on how to hear God's voice that I encourage you to read if you are not yet familiar with two-way journaling and vision. This teaching is extremely helpful to activating angelic encounters in your life because with both exercises you are interacting with spirit beings in another dimension.

Biblical Safeguards

As we get started on this journey into the sacred supernatural, we can be confident in our path by establishing some ground rules. We don't need to worry about being deceived by the enemy or even ourselves by simply putting some spiritual precautions in place.

Just as with hearing God's voice, engaging the angelic realm can almost seem *too* simple at times. Thoughts and pictures may come so easily, you question if they are divinely inspired and wonder how you know that it is not just your own imagination. And even more importantly, you want to know how to protect yourself from satan potentially getting you off track.

The answer to both of these critical questions is found in these five biblical safeguards.

1. You are a born-again Christian, having accepted Jesus Christ into your heart as your Lord and Savior and having your sins washed away by His cleansing blood.[16]

2. You accept the Bible as the inerrant Word of God.

3. You demonstrate your love and respect for God by your commitment to knowing His Word.

4. You have an attitude of submission to what God has shown you from the Bible.

5. You have two or three spiritual advisors to whom you go for input on a regular basis.

If you answer *Yes* to all of the above, you are safe. You can confidently enter the spirit realm through Jesus knowing He is with you and is excited to show you around His world!

On occasion, people will tell me they have a friend who doesn't want to interact with angels because they used to be involved in witchcraft or the New Age and are worried of being deceived again. How do we know for sure these are holy angels?

Again, we use our guardrails for safe spiritual navigation, and this is exactly what I would ask:

- Was your friend a born-again, Spirit-filled Christian when she was engaging the angels?

- Was she reading her Bible and regularly fellowshipping with other believers?

- Was she obedient to what God had shown her in Scripture and living a lifestyle that demonstrated Christ's Lordship in her heart?

- Was she praying daily and focusing on her relationship with Jesus during that season in her life?

- Was she submitting the angelic messages to her spiritual advisors for confirmation?

- Did the angels direct her to Jesus? Did they talk about Father God? Did they remind her of Scriptures and explain things to her from the Bible, thereby continually re-focusing her on Christ and His Word?

In every case of deception, the answer was *No* to many if not all of these "red-flag" questions, so it's easy to understand how the person got involved with the wrong angels. Proverbs 11:14 promises us that in a multitude of counselors there is safety. God has established spiritual advisors as an umbrella of protection, to help guard us from self-deception within our own hearts, as well as from deception by the enemy.

This checklist helps us test the spirits to easily discern whether they are faithful or fallen. If we have met these simple requirements, we know we can continue moving forward into the sacred supernatural in freedom and without fear.

We Don't Have to Wait

The misunderstanding is that we usually think seeing angels is a special "encounter" that happens rarely and is an out-of-the-ordinary experience. We may hear exciting stories of a stranded motorist aided by a helpful passerby who then disappeared before he could be thanked, or a child being rescued by a stranger who happened to be at the right place at the right time. In these cases, there is often no explanation except for supernatural intervention. Praise God! We share some of these amazing testimonies later in the book, and we are very grateful for them!

Usually these stories are about angels who take on the form of a human and assist us. They physically come into our world, look like a person, and we see them with our natural eyes in our material realm.

Indeed, angels come to us this way, as they did throughout Scripture. The Bible often refers to angels as men who talked and ate food and looked very much like us. Of course, this is how we entertain them unaware; they seem so human we don't even recognize that they are angels (see Heb. 13:2)!

However, first and foremost, angels are spirit beings who live in the spirit realm. That is why, if we are waiting around for them to leave their spiritual world and put on flesh and come to our material realm, it could take a while. If we are waiting for them to come to us, it may be why we don't see them very often (if ever). We are insisting that they conform to our three-dimensional world.

What would happen if we stepped into their world instead of waiting around for those spiritual beings to come into our physical world? We are spiritual beings, too, and we have spiritual eyes. Paul prayed that the eyes of our hearts would be opened (see Eph. 1:17-18). We have spiritual senses that can see and hear in the heavenly realm, and if we look to see with those spiritual eyes we can see angels all the time.

Angels may appear to come and go, because we are looking at the physical world. Yes, they do move in and out of this natural dimension, but they don't go far! They only move back into their spiritual, heavenly dimension, that which is merely invisible but not distant from us. If we are looking only with our natural eyes, they appear to have left us.

That is why Paul prayed for our spiritual eyes to be opened and he told us to look at the unseen (see 2 Cor. 4:18). When we do that, we will see the truth. We will see that the angels never left, and they are still here with us. Jesus, Father, Holy Spirit, our angelic guardians—they are all here. The company of Heaven is not far off. It is only our limited perception and spiritual blindness that makes it seem that way.

Flashes of Light

This is why angels sometimes appear as flashes of light or color, without the form or body we would expect. If we look with our physical eyes, we will not see their fullness. Often, we will not perceive super-natural phenomena with our natural senses. It can happen, to be sure, but it is more common to sense the spirit with our spiritual faculties. So that flash of light or color is simply all that is manifesting in this mate-rial dimension. But if we set our attention and focus on the spirit world, their complete figure and form will come into view.

Imagine me standing outside a car you are sitting in. I stick my hand through the window to wave and you exclaim, "There's Charity!"

Well, that is true. It is me. But, obviously, my hand is not all of me. It is just all of me you can see from the vantage point of sitting in your car and looking straight ahead. However, if you turn your head and look out the window, you will see more of me. If you actually get out of your car and enter the dimension outside the car, you will get to see me fully and experience all of me. This example is not unlike the hand writing on the wall in Daniel 5. Was it a disembodied hand? Or was the hand just the only part of the spiritual body that was visible in this dimension? When we step into the sacred supernatural by looking with the eyes of our hearts, we will get to see angels more fully and com-pletely than if we just wait for them to manifest in this space-time world to our physical senses.

So We Can See Angels All the Time?

Yes! By looking for them where they live, in the supernatural realm. When we look to see with our spiritual eyes, and tune into that heavenly dimension, we will see that we are never alone. Jesus never leaves us. Our angels always have our back. And seeing this truth changes everything!

Remember when Elisha's servant was afraid of the enemy armies? He was looking only with his natural eyes at the natural realm. From that vantage point, things seemed overwhelming. He wasn't taking into account the heavenly armies that were on their side, so he was scared (see 2 Kings 6:15-17).

Then Elisha prayed that his servant's eyes would be opened to see the supernatural world and the angelic hosts that were encamped around them with heavenly protection. When Elisha's servant looked into the invisible realm and lived to that reality, fear left him. Hope and faith flooded his heart. He saw the truth that there were more with them than were against them!

When we see God's version of our situations, we will feel how God feels—His Kingdom emotions. God is never stressed out or overwhelmed. When we have His perspective, we won't be stressed out or overwhelmed either. This is our loving Father's heart for us: peace and joy in His Spirit. That's the Kingdom of God!

As believers, our spirit has been joined to Holy Spirit (see 1 Cor. 6:17). As such, we have the gifts of His Spirit available to us. One of these gifts is the discerning of spirits, which helps us to see and discern our guardian angels, our ministering spirits (see 1 Cor. 12:10).

While we have this gift available to us, it is important to "unwrap" the gift and activate it. How do we become better at discerning spirits? The same way we become skilled at anything: practice. The book of Hebrews tells us that "the mature, because of practice, have their senses trained to discern" (Heb. 5:14). If we're not discerning as much as we'd like, practicing will definitely help.

Seeing in the spirit is like dream interpretation. These are not special gifts bestowed on only a few, favored individuals. Seeing in the spirit—both by day and by night through dreams—is a skill that can be learned and strengthened by investing time and focused energy into it. Reading this book will help activate your perception and discernment of the angelic in your life.

Eyes Wide Open

Again, the steps we take to connect with Jesus and hear His voice spontaneously in our thoughts are the same steps we take to listen to our angels. We see and hear angels the same way we see and hear Jesus—by using the eyes and ears of our heart.[17]

When most of us experience the supernatural realm, we do not perceive it with our physical senses. Usually, when we say that we heard God or an angel speak to us, we don't mean that we heard an audible voice. Instead, we are often describing a spontaneous, flowing thought that comes to us as we focus our spiritual eyes on the company of Heaven—Jesus and His angels.

Similarly, when I say that I "talk with" my angels, I am not actually speaking out loud. They are spirits and can sense my spirit. Sometimes when there is a situation that requires angelic intervention, I only have to look their way and think "Guys...." And then I have a spontaneous thought back from them, "We're on it." They know what I mean, because supernatural communication is often expressed thought to thought, intention to intention, and heart to heart. Jesus knew in His spirit what the teachers of the law were thinking in their hearts (see Mark 2:8).

We are spirit beings, and we don't always need words to communicate. We know God hears our prayers even when they aren't verbalized. We are created in the image of God, who is Spirit (see John 4:24). We are spiritual beings designed for the spirit realm, so we purpose to awaken our spiritual eyes and ears. Because what is the alternative of living tuned into these supernatural senses?

Blindness. Spiritually we were blind and deaf, but Jesus came to open the eyes of the blind and unstop the deaf ears. Of course, this speaks to both physical healing and spiritual healing. God does not want us in spiritual darkness any longer!

It reminds me of playing peek-a-boo with small children. When they cover their eyes, they think you really do cease to exist. We have inadvertently done the same thing with the angelic realm. Just because we don't see them, does not mean they are not there. Jesus Himself actually called us to be seers and witnesses.

Witness Defined

After Jesus died, was buried, rose from the grave, and then returned to earth, He gave His disciples some final instructions. Right before He ascended to Heaven, Jesus told them to wait for the promise of the Father. The very last thing someone says before they leave is important. The last thing Jesus said was, "Guys, don't go anywhere until you've been baptized with the Holy Spirit."

Now why would that be? Jesus went on to explain that this experience would give them power to be His witnesses (see Acts 1:1-8). Jesus said that once Holy Spirit comes and baptizes us, we are empowered to be witnesses of Jesus.

Christians often think of witnessing as something we do with our mouth; yet, most people associate the word witness with vision. That's the dictionary definition: we personally see something; we are onlookers who observe. Eyewitness News shows us the story from the perspective of someone who saw the event firsthand. If we are called as a witness in a courtroom, we saw a crime or an accident take place. Or if we "witness history in the making" it is because the commentator believes that we saw an extraordinary feat take place right before our eyes. In order to be a witness, we must be an observer and a seer.

Jesus taught us that the baptism of the Holy Spirit opens the eyes of our hearts to the supernatural world that is all around us. It unlocks the spiritual dimension to us, so we have the power to see the spirit realm that permeates and infuses the physical realm. Holy Spirit anoints us to observe the Kingdom of God that is so close, it's within us (see Luke 17:21 KJV).

We know this is how Jesus lived. He said "I do nothing on my own initiative. I only do what I see the Father do and say what I hear Him say" (see John 5:19-20, 30; 8:38). In order to model Jesus, we need to be able to see what He and Father are doing, and hear what Holy Spirit is saying. We want to partner with our angels by not being blind to them. Right now, we're real-time witnesses and present-tense observers of the activity of Heaven. That is what Jesus was talking about in Acts 1:8.

The Secret

Holy Spirit baptism enables us to fix our eyes on Jesus (see Heb. 12:2). It allows us to set our mind on the spirit (see Rom. 8:5-6) and equips us to see angels in the invisible realm (see 2 Cor. 4:18). We receive power when the Holy Spirit has come upon us to be His witnesses. Witnesses of Jesus. Seers of Jesus. Lookers and watchers and observers of Jesus. Jesus wants a witness to His life—the one He's living right now.

And Jesus isn't alone! He is surrounded by the company of Heaven, the angelic hosts. It is significant that God identifies Himself so closely with angels. In Scripture, He often refers to Himself as the "Lord of Hosts." The word "hosts" means armies and refers to His angelic armies. This gives us a glimpse into God's heart for angels. He doesn't distance Himself from them. He doesn't downplay them as lowly ministering servants. He honors angels by calling Himself by their name: Lord of Hosts!

Since He loves angels so much, doesn't it show our heart for God when we love them, too? We care about what He cares about. We honor who He honors. We esteem the Giver when we appreciate and value His gift.

In summary, we see that the baptism of the Holy Spirit empowers us to be witnesses of the company of Heaven and observers of the sacred supernatural. If you haven't been baptized by Holy Spirit yet and want to be, just ask Him. You can also check out our resources on how to be filled with the Spirit and power, including my dad's free video teaching on praying in tongues.[18] It is easier than you think! In fact, it all starts with being a follower of Jesus. If you want to be closer to Him, read Appendix A to learn how.

Let Holy Spirit open the eyes of your heart to the Kingdom of God that is upon you, within you, and all around you. Thank You, Father, for the gift of sight. We once were blind but now we see!

Next Steps

What if you are already a Spirit-filled Christian, but you are still not seeing angels as often as you would like? Well, obviously, the more we look, the more we will see. And there is a big difference between quickly glancing around to look for angels, and fixing our spiritual eyes and purposefully gazing into the supernatural realm looking for them. We tend to use the word "look" rather loosely. Scripture talks about "looking intently" and "fixing our eyes" and "setting our mind" upon the spirit, which is more than a swift superficial scan.

So we become intent on seeing the realms of Heaven. But where do we look for that?

Where's Heaven?

The revelation is that Heaven is all around us. The spirit realm is right here. The supernatural infuses the natural. Christ is all and in all and in Him all things hold together (see Col. 1:17; 3:11). We know Christ is Spirit, so it is spirit that is holding all of this seemingly solid physical world together.[19]

We might be tempted to think Heaven is a few billion light years away, far off in a distant galaxy somewhere. But Jesus said the Kingdom of Heaven is at hand (see Matt. 10:7). The Kingdom has come near you (see Luke 10:9). The Kingdom is in your midst; it is within you (see Luke 17:21). I'm not really sure how many other ways He could tell us, "It's here! It's now! Live into Heaven and live out of it."

Scripture says that God "makes His angels winds" (see Heb. 1:7). One obvious characteristic of wind is that you can't see it. Wind can be strong and powerful. It can cool and refresh us on a hot summer's day. Wind, however, is still invisible.

Similarly, our angelic bodyguards are strong and powerful. They can refresh and minister to us, and they too are not usually seen with our natural eyes. We can be comfortable and confident with this invisible arrangement, knowing that God makes His angels winds, so even though we don't always see them physically, they are still very real, relevant, and right here with us.

The spiritual realm of Heaven is just like magnetic fields, radio waves, and Wi-Fi signals—it is invisible. But just because we can't see any of those things doesn't mean they're not surrounding us all the time and literally permeating our atmosphere.

What God Wants Us to Know

Indeed, it is significant to notice the very first recorded words of Jesus' public ministry. What does He say before anything else? Matthew 4:17 tells us: "Repent!"

The Greek word for repent is *metanoeó* and it means to think differently. To repent is to change your mind, to literally think differently afterwards. Jesus is telling us to get a new mindset. See differently than we have been. Change our thinking.

Sure thing, Jesus. We can do that! So what is it that we need to think differently about? What are You telling us to get a new understanding and revelation about?

Jesus explained, "The Kingdom of Heaven is near" (Matt. 4:17).

He is saying, "Hey, you know that Heaven you've been looking for? It has arrived. That Kingdom you've been waiting for? It's here right now actually. It is not far off, way in the distance and separate from you. It is close by! Adjust your thinking. See the truth! The Kingdom of Heaven is here. The Kingdom of Heaven is at hand. The Kingdom of Heaven has come near you. The Kingdom of Heaven is in your midst!

"You had been thinking God was far off. You had been seeing Heaven as the sweet by and by, a future place that is very much removed from your everyday existence. And that's where you missed it. That's what I've come to change. In fact, it is so important that it is the very first thing I'm going to announce and declare. The very first message I'm going to preach to the world. Get a new understanding, guys. Wrap your mind around this!

"The Kingdom of Heaven is here, and the Kingdom of Heaven is now."

Just Like Elijah

To summarize, we have learned that we can use the four keys to hear both the voice of God and the voice of angels. We recognize that this voice will not often be loud and audible, but a still, small voice that comes as spontaneous thoughts when our spiritual eyes are fixed on Heaven.

Just as Elijah expected to hear God's voice in the earthquake or the storm, and was surprised that God's voice was gentle and quiet, so too are the subtle exchanges with our angels (see 1 Kings 19:11-13). And this is actually a good thing! If God and His angels are not shouting loudly, that is a positive sign. We only raise our voice with someone if they are not listening to us or if they are far away. The fact that the company of Heaven can simply whisper in our hearts shows that we are spiritually tuned in and paying attention. It is a compliment that God can speak to us in such a low key way and we can hear Him clearly. Be encouraged, you are on the right track!

Sometimes, listening is the easier skill to develop, and you may have angelic conversations in the thoughts of your heart before you actually see your angels. That's okay and is a great place to start!

In the next chapter, we will build on these foundational principles of listening in the spirit and add even more tools to our belt. We will explore the importance of imagination and other secrets of the seers, as well as several actionable steps we can take to tune into the frequency of Heaven.

What About You?

- Read John 3:1-17. Have you been born from above as a follower of Christ? If you are not completely sure of your salvation, you can be. Simply read and pray through Appendix A *How to Be Born of the Spirit* and visit www.BornOfTheSpirit.Today.

- Read Luke 24:49 and Acts 1:1-8. Have you received the baptism of the Holy Spirit? Would you like to be "clothed with power from on high"? Experience teaching and activation on how to speak in tongues: www.cwgministries.org/tonguesvideo.

- Do you easily and regularly have two-way journaling conversations with God? If not, read Appendix B.

- Do you have all five biblical safeguards for spirit realm navigation in place in your life? How do you think they will help protect you on your journey into the sacred supernatural?

Chapter 12

Angelic Activation:
How to See in the Spirit

by Charity Kayembe

Now we understand the amazing world of the spirit that Jesus wants us to join Him in, the biggest question becomes, how do we get there? The essential basics include being a Christ follower, being baptized by His Spirit, and learning to discern and recognize what His voice sounds like, but there is more we can do.

Godly Imagination

To see in the spirit we will use one of the best gifts God ever gave us: our imagination. We are created in God's image and we have an imagination because God has an imagination! My dad, Mark Virkler writes,

I believe our imagination is one of the ways in which we most strongly reflect God's image. By it we can create our own heaven or hell on earth. By it, we can be co-creators with Him, releasing His Kingdom on earth as it is in Heaven. If we truly trust in Him, our imagination will steadfastly see and frame up and form all He has promised to us, and nothing else.[20]

God discusses imagination in Scripture, but often the word has been mistranslated in the English, so we have missed what He's saying. For example, most of us are familiar with the promise in Isaiah 26:3—"The steadfast of mind You will keep in perfect peace, because he trusts in You."

However, according to *Brown-Driver-Briggs Hebrew Lexicon*, the word "mind" is translated from the Hebrew word *yêtser* (Strong's #H3336) and means "imagination, which forms and frames up." Therefore a more accurate rendering of the passage would be:

"The steadfast of imagination You will keep in perfect peace, because he trusts in You."

Having a steadfast or godly imagination is picturing things that God says are so. We set the scene and imagine it, then invite Holy Spirit to enlighten the eyes of our hearts (see Eph. 1:18). Our imagination is not a supernatural vision; it is just a stepping-stone into the vision (see Acts 2:17). When we tune to flow, we will see God take over the scene and bring it alive (see John 7:37-39). That is when we know it is no longer our imagined scene, but now a revelatory vision from Heaven.

Apostolic minister and prophetic voice Patricia King reveals more about the importance of using our imagination in her wonderful book *Eyes That See*:

The faint impressions in the mind and imagination are the most common ways God reveals vision to His people. Often believers do not feel this is a significant vision and that it is a lower level than perhaps an open vision. This is not true. There are no lower or higher levels or types of vision. They are simply different ways that God uses to reveal His will and purpose. Each way is precious if God is the source.

Most seasoned and credible prophets will confirm that the most predominant ways that God speaks to them is through the still small God-thoughts in the mind and the faint impressions in the imagination.[21]

This confirms precisely what I have found as I have talked with friends and ministers who see in the spirit. I specifically ask them how defined and "concrete" the angels are that they see, and almost everyone agrees on their transparent nature. After all, they are spirits.

Most of us do not often have "open visions" where we see things with our natural eyes. We usually have "closed visions," where our physical eyes are closed and we're seeing with our spiritual eyes. Things seen in the supernatural are usually less "solid" and three-dimensional.

Katie Souza, founder of Expected End Ministries, shares about the "Angel Spies" who showed up in her kitchen one evening wearing safari outfits. Complete with hats, maps and binoculars, she too confirmed that "they were transparent, not solid. I could see them and see through them at the same time."[22]

I sometimes describe it as seeing "the idea" of an angel.

Superimposed Supernatural

For example, think back to your last vacation. Imagine that favorite beach or restaurant and how much you enjoyed it! Now, that picture is fairly clear in your mind's eye, isn't it? You have a definite memory of it and you can see that place in your imagination. However, it is not as firm and strong as the book you are holding in your hands. It is not as concrete as this natural world, but it is still real. You can still see it and remember it and even describe that picture.

And so it is with angels.

More often than not, they are quite see-through and appear almost overlaid on the physical world. Take a look at the front cover of this book. See how the angel is superimposed over the ocean? This was intentional as we want to give you a glimpse of how the supernatural realm gently engages the natural realm. When we know what we're looking for, it is easier to see. So not only are angelic voices quieter than we might expect, their forms are normally less defined than we would expect as well. And usually, whether our natural eyes are open or closed, we will be able to see right through them. This is a common experience, and for me, this is how angels appear. So, look for the faint picture. Focus on the transparent image. And more than anything, honor it. Honor what you see by paying attention to it.

Whatever we are grateful for we get more of. Even if you only glimpse a hazy appearance at first, purpose to honor the little that you do see, and trust your spiritual eyesight will strengthen with exercise. Whatever we honor, we empower. Whatever we place our attention and focus and energy on, we increase and release more of into our lives.

How Daniel Saw

Even Daniel, the great prophetic seer in Scripture, had closed visions. He records not only what he saw, but how he saw it. Over and over he describes these heavenly pictures as "visions in his mind" (see Dan. 7:1, 15). He made it a point to let us know that it was not an external experience. Daniel was using his spiritual eyes and spiritual ears to experience the spiritual Kingdom within (see Luke 17:21).

His life was filled with exciting visions of angels and it is no secret why. The Bible makes it clear that he saw and saw and saw because he looked and looked and looked (see Dan. 7:2, 4, 6, 7, 9, 11, 13). Zechariah's extended visionary conversation with an angel is described in a similar way. He kept on looking, too (see Zech. 1:18; 2:1; 5:1).

And in Revelation John said the same thing, "I looked and behold...," "I looked and I saw...," "I looked and I heard the voice of many angels..." (see Rev. 4:1; 5:11; 6:2, 5, 8; 7:9; 8:13; et al.).

While this may seem obvious, it cannot be overstated: taking the time to look is a definite key to seeing! I don't mean a quick glance. I mean we should fix our spiritual eyes, gaze intently, and focus on the spirit realm without distraction.

I don't see angels all the time, but I do see them whenever I look. I don't see much in the natural realm with my eyes closed either. So, in the same way I need to continually pray that the eyes of my heart be wide open and enlightened, I need to be looking to see what I can see (see Eph. 1:18).

One more thing to be aware of is that many people will sense angels and may not see them right away. That is okay, too! If you are aware of an angel's presence, honor that feeling. If you are seeing a faint image, honor that vision. If you are hearing a quiet thought, honor that voice.

As I have led people into angelic activation, hearing has often come before seeing as well. Especially with those familiar with hearing God's voice and two-way journaling, it is easy for them to pick up spontaneous thoughts from the spirit world. The natural next step is to simply ask Jesus to make some angelic introductions. Every time I have asked, He is more than happy to do so!

Charlette's Angels

For instance, I serve as Vice President of Academic Affairs at Christian Leadership University and one of our graduate students, Charlette, wanted to meet her angels. In my office she quieted down, looked for vision, and tuned into the spontaneous impressions that bubbled up from her heart.

The most amazing thing happened when she asked Jesus about her angels. He immediately and gladly introduced her to them, and then He left! One would have thought Jesus would want to oversee their conversation, make sure the angels stayed in line, or ensure she didn't start worshiping them.

On the contrary, we were both surprised when Jesus walked over to the other side of the room, essentially giving Charlette time to get to know her guardian angels a little better on her own. No divine micro-management required. Again, this shows how secure God is and how He's not threatened by our healthy friendships. We can have relationships with others beyond Him, and that includes angels. He's not controlling. He encourages these angelic partnerships!

Secrets of the Seers

There are some members of the body of Christ who are the "eyes"—the seers. They will be the more right-brained, intuitive, visionary creatives among us. And they will tend to see more clearly than the rest of us.

However, even the late prophetic seer Bob Jones revealed that his visions were often faint pictures in his imagination. They were usually never as bright, clear, or solid as what he saw in the natural world. Bob said that all prophecy begins in the imagination, and when he took people to Heaven in the spirit he started by having them picture the scene. That was the stepping-stone. Then Holy Spirit breathed on the natural imagination and transformed it into a supernatural vision.

This is an encouragement for us! Bob honored those spontaneous thoughts and pictures until he was confident they were images from Heaven, and we can do that, too. Indeed, for many right-brained, intuitive people the problem is not that they don't see angels. It is that they see them too easily!

Prophetic visionaries often find that when they close their eyes, they see. However, they immediately discount the picture as their own imagination without honoring it long enough for God to take over the scene by continuing to look. When we come to God, we must come in faith, which means we honor what we see (see Heb. 11:6).

As always, everything we experience must line up with Scriptural principles. In addition, the best way to gain confidence that we're actually receiving revelation from Heaven is to simply share our experiences with our spiritual advisors and let them confirm it. Most often they will tell us that what the angel said or did was unexpected and much more wise and compassionate than we naturally are! This is what we want to hear because it confirms the encounter was not just us making it up, but indeed supernatural.

Recovering Sight

We all have spiritual eyes, and we can all see. Nobody is left out. God does not intend for some of us to see and others to be blind. Jesus came to bring "recovery of sight to the blind" (see Luke 4:18). The Greek phrase used in this verse is the same one used in Mark 6:41 where it says Jesus "lifted up His eyes to Heaven."

Essentially in the original language it says that Jesus "recovered His sight." When we look into Heaven, we see God's version of the situation and recover His perspective. We see what God sees, His reality and point of view. We recover our spiritual eyesight, seeing that angels are here and waiting for us to partner with them, and we live to that truth.

This isn't a competition. We are not comparing ourselves to our brothers and sisters in the body of Christ, because when we measure ourselves against others we are without knowledge. Instead, we are grateful for whatever we can see and we purpose to exercise the eyes of our hearts to increase their spiritual discernment, knowing that our senses will be trained with practice (see Heb. 5:14).

Heart-Based Living

Remember how Charlette quieted herself down to pick up on her heart's sensations? This is important. We want to get out of our heads and into our hearts because God does not live in our heads. Ephesians 3:17 tells us that Jesus lives in our hearts and John 7:37-39 tells us that rivers of living water—the Holy Spirit—flow from deep within. As believers, we know that our spirit is joined with Holy Spirit deep down in our innermost being.

Therefore, we want to live from our hearts and our spirits, from down deep, from our union with God there. When we are in this sacred place, scientifically speaking, we are in the alpha brainwave state.

As you are wide awake, reading this book, and engaging your mind, you are in the faster analytical beta brainwave state. However, just as you fall asleep at night, and just as you wake up in the morning, you are in the alpha brainwave state.

This slower frequency state is more meditative and reflective. When we are not quite sure if we are awake or asleep, the veil between the physical world and spiritual world is very thin and we are in the alpha brainwave state. We are also in this brainwave frequency when we dream.

While science calls this alpha brainwaves, Scripture calls it being "in spirit." Jesus told us to "worship in spirit" (see John 4:24). John said "I was in spirit on the Lord's day" and met with God (see Rev. 1:10ff). Again, he said "I was in spirit" and proceeded to see Father's throne and all manner of heavenly vision (see Rev. 4:2ff). He was not in his head. He was in his heart. He wasn't in beta. He was in alpha, and that is when his spiritual senses were opened wide to see and hear the mysteries of the Kingdom.

Angel Dreams

We can see how important dreams are as an effective communicative medium with Heaven. When we receive dreams, our analytical mind is out of the way, and we are able to receive a pure flow of revelation straight from Father's heart to ours. Indeed, Scripture reveals that when we are asleep, our heart is awake to commune with our Beloved (see Song of Sol. 5:2).

Dreams are God's contingency plan to ensure He always has a way to connect with us. Father knows that the best time to get our undistracted attention is during sleep. Throughout Scripture, God used dreams to enlighten and encourage, and at times He delivered these directional messages through the ministry of angels.

Over and over in the Gospel of Matthew, angels brought specific instructions to Joseph, the earthly father of Jesus, while he slept. In a dream, an angel told Joseph to take Mary as his wife (see Matt. 1:20-24). Joseph moved his family to Egypt to escape Herod because an angel told him to in a dream (see Matt. 2:13-14). Later, he moved Jesus and Mary back to Israel because an angel told him to in a dream (see Matt. 2:19-21).

These were critical directions intended to protect baby Jesus from being killed. You would think God might want Joseph awake for such important revelation. Or, at the very least you would think God might want to speak to Joseph personally, since the stakes were so high. But God chose to use dreams and angels to communicate His messages, and He still does the same today. We can be comfortable and confident about meeting angels while we sleep, because Scripture demonstrates that dreams are bridges to the supernatural.

10 Ways to Get "in Spirit"

But what about when we are awake? Obviously, we want to receive heavenly revelation all day long, too. Are there any other ways we can position ourselves to receive more readily from the supernatural realm?

Absolutely! Just like the reflection on a cellphone or computer screen—different angles and amounts of light illuminate what is being shown. When there are high levels of light in the room, we need to increase the brightness of the display in order to see more than just reflections on the screen.

In a similar way, we can increase the brightness of the vision-ary screen inside our hearts. We do this by moving into the alpha brainwave state. Science has demonstrated there are practical and proven ways we can slow down our brain waves. Founder of Impact

Ministries, Dr. James Richards shares several in his book, *Moving Your Invisible Boundaries*:

> It is interesting that so many of the physical forms of worship tend to slow down our brain waves. Music is very instrumental in effecting our brain waves. Chanting, which is done in many of the Psalms and is actually used in the Hebrew language to describe worship, slows the brain waves. Rolling our eyes up, as if looking to heaven, rocking, singing songs with repeated rhythmic patterns, bowing, dancing and pretty much all of the physical expressions of praise and worship, slow the brain waves.
>
> When this happens we think that God, who lives way off in heaven has suddenly been appeased to such a degree that He graces us with His presence. But the truth is just the opposite; God, who lives in us and is always expressing Himself to us, is finally realized by the shift in our awareness. We begin to experience what He has been expressing all along![23]

This is similar to how the discipline of fasting helps us tune in to hear from God. It is not that He is speaking more clearly when we fast; it's simply that we have positioned ourselves to hear Him better. So it is with these various ways to worship and meditate: They don't change God; they change us!

We instinctively do many of these things to naturally quiet down an upset baby. We rock them gently, sway back and forth, and sing songs to them. We know these are effective ways to settle down a child, and now we recognize that they are also effective ways to quiet ourselves down, to settle us into our hearts and spirits.

We see this exemplified in Scripture with the prophet Elisha. When he wanted to receive a revelation from God he also used the tool of music: "'But now bring me a minstrel.' And it came about, when the minstrel played, that the hand of the LORD came upon him" and he received a prophetic word to declare (see 2 Kings 3:15ff).

While it may go without saying, closing our eyes is obviously another simple and effective way to shift our awareness from the external to the internal. This also moves us down into that alpha state of spiritual sensitivity, so that we are less distracted by the outer world and more focused on the Kingdom within.

In Joshua 1:8, God told Israel's new up-and-coming leader how to be successful. The secret? Biblical meditation. Meditation moves us to the alpha/spirit level, giving us a greater sensitivity and awareness of the sacred supernatural. Soft soaking music and visionary prayer are excellent tools for this. My father and I unpack the extraordinary gift of meditation in our book on Kingdom emotions,[24] and I encourage you to experience the New Creation Celebration Meditations available free on his ministry website.[25]

Another extremely efficient way I have found to quiet myself down is through Emotional Freedom Techniques (EFT).[26] EFT, or "tapping" as it is often called, has been scientifically documented to consistently slow down our brain waves, bringing us into a place of calm and rest. It moves us from beta to alpha quickly and effortlessly, thus moving us from our heads to our hearts.

As a predominantly left-brain teacher, I naturally live in my head, therefore, I must manually shift gears and intentionally slow down into my heart. Hundreds of studies show the near-miraculous benefits of tapping, and I have co-developed training resources on it from a biblical perspective.[27,28] I use tapping as a tool to move me into my heart zone.

Again, because Jesus lives in my heart, I endeavor to live from my heart and the springs of His River of Life that flow from there (see Prov. 4:23).

Praying in tongues also moves us into the alpha state making us more aware of the spiritual realm and our connection to it. Supernatural leaders such as Sid Roth and Mahesh Chavda testify that their commitment to praying in the Spirit an hour a day unleashed tremendous power and anointing through their ministries.

Indeed, I have found that singing in the Spirit is one of the quickest ways for me to become aware of God's peace and presence. When we sing and pray in tongues, our spirit is praying (see 1 Cor. 14:14-15). Our spirit is one with Holy Spirit (see 1 Cor. 6:17). So we are connecting with Holy Spirit and allowing Him to pray with and through us (see Rom. 8:26-27).

Angelic Introductions

Now that you know what to do and how to do it, let's return to the question of how to meet your angels: Simply have a conversation with Jesus and ask Him to make some angelic introductions!

You have several options for quieting yourself down and getting "in spirit." Once in your heart, listen for what you can hear and look for what you can see. An excellent tool for accomplishing this is the visionary prayer experience, "Angel Introductions," available free online.[29]

Accompanied by soaking music in the background, you are guided to picture yourself with Jesus using your godly imagination. Once you meet Him, He will transform your imagined picture into a supernatural vision. Honor the spontaneous flow of pictures and thoughts you receive when you ask Him questions, and you will begin having a conversation. Ask Jesus what He thinks of you, and how He sees you. Let

Him tell you how much He loves you and how proud He is of you. Spend a few minutes enjoying each other's company.

Then, you can ask Him some of the other questions you have on your heart: What would He like to share with you about angels? What does He want to show you? What does Jesus want you to know about the heavenly guardians He assigned to you, and would He like you to meet them right now?

I am confident He will be delighted to introduce you to your angelic companions, and they will be equally thrilled for you to finally make their acquaintance. They have been looking forward to this moment for your whole life! They can't wait for you to finally get to know them, too.

What About You?

- How do you tend to view your imagination? In light of what you learned in this chapter, has your perspective changed at all?

- Read Matthew chapters 1 and 2. How important was it that Joseph obeyed the angel in his dreams? What does this demonstrate about honoring our dreams? Have you ever received messages from God in your dreams? Did you act on them?

- Have you met with Jesus and your angels yet? If not, use the free "Angel Introductions" meditation at GloryWaves.org/Angels and ask Jesus if He'd like to help you make their acquaintance.

- What was your experience?

Chapter 13

Paris: The Watcher on the Eiffel Tower

by Joe Brock

I want to share one last story where I had a life-changing interaction with a massive angel. In truth, this story was the very first trip I took that involved angels. I wanted to save the best for last.

The story itself begins with a stirring of the Lord. Each journey I have made has started with the Lord getting my attention, which leads me to wait on Him until plans begin to materialize. I felt His leading and it drew me into His presence where He began to speak to me things I had never heard before.

Divine Dialogue, Blessed Confirmations, and the Matrix

The Lord told me to travel to France, to the first level of the Eiffel Tower. There I was to release an angel who would stand as a guardian and watcher until the end of time.

I will freely admit that hearing something like this for the first time can stretch your faith and belief system as few other things can. The Lord told me that He had assigned to me angels that I could commission to assist me in fulfilling the various missions He would continue to send me on.

Because of the nature of what I felt I was hearing I did not share this openly until some type of confirmation came. A short time later I received a phone call from a friend living 500 miles away.

This friend of mine had been attending a Sunday night teaching series about angels at his church. The speaker was an itinerate minister who said he believed that God had delegated angels to each of us and they have nothing to do until their human counterpart gives them an assignment. My friend called to see what my feelings were on this topic.

What an incredible, maturing moment for me. This was the confirmation I was waiting for. The Lord told me to release an angel and to give it an assignment. He then pushed my worldview even farther by telling me that He had assigned angels to co-labor with me to fulfill my calling. I was shocked and waited for confirmation, which came through the phone call of a friend who lived 500 miles away and who wanted to know my opinion about angels waiting for their assignments. Once I received this confirmation, I moved forward in obedience, even though I had never stepped out in faith like this before.

Interestingly enough, through the "Matrix Reloaded" movie, the Lord taught me a valuable lesson. Commander Jason Locke was addressing the Zion Council about an impending danger. The Council requested two ships be sent to look for Neo's spaceship thus leaving the last human city, Zion, with an increased defenselessness. In response, Commander Locke told the council he couldn't comprehend their decision to put the city at greater risk by asking fighter ships to depart on a fruitless mission.

Councilor West replied: "Comprehension is not a requisite of cooperation." What great wisdom!

There is so much truth in this. Pure obedience is based on our willingness, regardless of our comprehension of a situation. To *need* information or to *have to comprehend* makes us the one in charge, and thus takes away the genuine nature of obedience. When God tells us to do something, whether He explains it or not, our willingness to obey lies purely in our hands. When God says go, we go, because we love and trust Him.

Funds and Passports

As the trip began to unfold and the time was getting closer, the money to fund the trip had not arrived. When I first started making these trips, I would send out letters soliciting money. As time went on, I began to see that if God called me to do something, God would make it happen. This includes finances. This was an awkward thing for me because I did not know God well enough to know His ways in moments like this. Since then, God has taught me that He will send the money to me and often in creative ways.

A friend of mine found out I was preparing for this trip. He was a successful businessman and brother in the Lord and he contacted me to ask about the mission. I shared what I felt like I could without freaking him out too much. He listened intently and at the end of the conversation asked, "How much do you need?" I had run the numbers and for airfare, transportation, the time at the hotel, meals, and so on, the cost came close to thirty-five hundred dollars. He answered, "The check will be in the mail tomorrow." Just like that the money was there, and I was able to make all my travel arrangements. Getting the passport would be another whole issue.

When the Lord told me about the Paris trip, my first passport was about to expire. I took steps to get another one in time for my trip. At this point in our lives, I pastored a church in the southwest corner of Virginia. My parents lived in Northern Indiana, so when I traveled, my wife and kids would stay with my folks, and I would fly out of Chicago.

While waiting for my passport, the days turned into weeks. Keep in mind that the non-refundable tickets for the flight and hotel were paid for by a friend, but without a passport I was not going anywhere. Just two weeks before the trip, I still had no passport.

I happened to have a phone conversation with the man who paid for the trip. I shared with him all that was happening and that the passport should have been at my home weeks prior. He told me to call my local government officials and let them know what was going on. I called, and they assured me they would investigate the matter immediately. I got a phone call back within a day from a young lady who told me they found the documentation for the new passport lying on a shelf. She assured me the passport would be processed and shipped immediately.

My flight was on a Monday, so we intended to travel to Indiana a few days early so I could rest before I flew to France. I woke up the day we were to drive to Indiana overflowing with fear and trembling. We lived on a rural mail route, and our mailbox was up a path from our home. I made my way to that mailbox numerous times looking for the mail and my much-needed package.

The mail lady finally arrived, but no passport came with her. I tried to trust, but truth be told, I was a mess. After I picked up the mail and walked back to our home, I was angry, frustrated, confused, and worried. What would I say to the man who paid for a trip I would not be able to go on? I went into the house and just fell on the couch not knowing what to do.

As I sat there in this state of emotional chaos, I heard a car pull up our gravel road. Our home sat back in the woods, surrounded by trees, and we had no visible neighbors. When we received company, we could hear them drive down the long gravel driveway.

I looked out the window and saw a personally owned car with a large plastic sign attached to it that read U.S. MAIL. Jubilation time! The mail lady pulled up and got out of her car. She walked up on the porch and was greeted by a very enthusiastic man. She apologized and said she had a package that was special delivery and forgot to drop it off when she was by earlier. I grabbed the packet, tore it open, and there was my passport! I was going to Paris after all.

God Is Never Arbitrary

I wondered why God would do that. I have come to know over the years that God is not arbitrary. Nothing is meaningless or without purpose. The word disciple means a taught one or one who is being trained.

As the days passed, I eventually understood what God was teaching me. Our pride is what leads us to live blind to the fact that we need God in every aspect of our human existence. The delay in the passport revealed to me that I trusted God with things I knew I couldn't do for myself. However, when I didn't think I needed God, I trusted myself. I felt that when things got difficult, I could often make things happen through my own efforts.

I thought I was trusting God with the passport, but when the panic set in, I realized I had been trusting in my own efforts. When the dust settled, I did get my passport, but it was because of God's intervention and not mine. Even though I was going through the process of preparing for a trip, God used this very method to disciple me in His ways. As painful and frustrating as these times are, they make it easier to trust in the future.

My New French Friends

We successfully made it to my folk's house, and the time arrived for me to travel to Chicago to catch my flight. In Northern Indiana, there is a commercial bus line that goes from various spots to the airports in Chicago. I intended to take this bus to O'Hare airport, where my departure flight was taking off.

Along the route, the bus makes several stops to pick people up and drop them off. My wife asked if I wanted to have her drive me to the next stop and catch the bus there. It was about an hour away, and doing so would give me that much extra time with her and my kids. I am sincerely in love with my wife and kids, so this was a very tempting offer. My heart, however, did not have peace about this.

There was a real struggle between my head and heart. My head said I should spend that extra time with my family, but my heart said I needed to get on the bus now. I told my wife as much as I wanted this extra time with them, I needed to get on the bus in South Bend. Within an hour, I understood why, and it was another precious gift from God.

I got on the bus and began to make myself comfortable. I looked around at the other passengers and settled in for a 3-hour ride. Over my left shoulder, I noticed a husband and wife sitting next to each other. As we traveled, I could hear them talk and I recognized they spoke with an accent. When we made our first passenger exchange stop, the person to my immediate left got off the bus. For some unknown reason, this husband and wife got up and moved up one seat so they were now sitting across from me.

As we continued our route to the airport, I could now clearly hear them talking with a French accent. After a few minutes, I leaned over and asked them if, in fact, they were French. They said yes, and I then asked where they were traveling to; they responded they were on their way to Paris. I shared with them that I, too, was going to Paris. We compared itineraries, and we were not only all going to Paris, but we were all seated on the same flight just a couple rows apart from each other.

I struck a deal with them. I would help them navigate through customs and the international terminal of O'Hare airport if they would help me once we arrived in Paris. They happily agreed. I had been to Charles de Gaulle Airport in Paris before and I remembered how large and complicated it was to navigate. On this particular trip, I was planning to go to the train station at the airport and take a train to my hotel. When I connected with this French couple, I saw the hand of my Father taking care of me. He orchestrated everything perfectly.

I helped this husband and wife through customs and we got to our flight in plenty of time. We had a great plane ride and arrived in Paris right on schedule. They graciously helped me through de Gaulle airport and walked me down to the train station. They even showed me where to stand for the exact train I needed. After hugs and goodbyes, my train arrived on time, and the train carried me to a station within a block of my hotel. It could not have worked out better.

Looking back at events like this amazes me. What are the odds of sitting next to a French couple that had been traveling through the U.S. for weeks? What if I ignored the Holy Spirit's prompting in my heart and got on the bus at a later stop? What are the odds of this French couple not only being next to me but taking the same exact flight and being seated within a few rows of me?

I dread to think how things would have gone for me without my Father's intervention. People have told me that things like this never happen to them. I tell them that if they want to see God's hands involved in their life, they must put their hands in their pockets. When you are in charge, God is not and when you are not, God is.

Time Is Drawing Near

Every trip that God sends me on is a unique experience. There are certain everyday things that happen on each trip—hearing God, seeking clarity on the assignment, and waiting on Him—but each trip has a distinct purpose.

On several of the trips I have taken, God has assigned an exact time I am to do what I am purposed to do. This set time will often coincide with a Bible verse. So, for instance, if I am to release God's love, He may have me pray at 3:16 in the afternoon and part of the prayer may include declaring John 3:16. This was on the agenda for this trip to Paris.

As I mentioned before, God was leading me to the lowest level of the Eiffel Tower. The Lord told me that when I got there, the Spirit would guide me to the exact spot I was to stand. At the exact minute God spoke to me about, I would release the angel to guard and watch until time ends. I was two days away from the day and time I was to fulfill this commission, so I took the opportunity to rest and make a "trial run" to get my bearings and be prepared.

The next day, the day before my assignment, I made a trip to the tower. It was just a short walk away. The size of the Eiffel Tower is indescribable; you must see it in person to truly grasp its enormity. For weeks leading up to the trip, I spent many mornings at a local walking track. When I saw how many steps I would have to climb to get to the lower level, I was pleased I put in the extra exercise.

After a couple of hours, I was satisfied with what I needed to do and how I was to accomplish it. I returned to my hotel and settled for the night. As the evening unfolded, and I lay before the Lord, there was a point the Lord took me into a vision where I saw a massive angel. In the vision, I knew the angel was close to 20 feet tall and though I could see him, he never did or said anything to me. I was not sure of the purpose of the vision or what the angel meant, but the next day it became amazingly clear.

The Time Has Arrived

I awoke the next morning ready to fulfill the Lord's calling. I left in plenty of time to get to the Eiffel Tower and for my daunting climb. I noticed that Europeans are in shape. They are not just thin, but they are in good physical form. I was somewhat concerned about climbing the 328 steps or 19 stories to the first level. The concern was not so much if I could make it, but I wondered about the pace I could keep. I did not want to have fit Europeans stuck behind me, with my very American build and speed.

God did me another favor. After I paid the fee to ascend, I made my way to the steps. Immediately in front of me were a man and wife beginning the journey upward. The woman was apparently afraid of heights. As I watched her, she would go up a step or two and stop and grab the hand railing with both hands. I am not sure what her husband said to her, but I am sure it would be classified under the 'do not say that' category you would teach your child. His chastising did not seem to faze her at all. She was going to climb at her own pace regardless of what her husband was saying. This was difficult for her but wonderful for me! God gave me the gift of climbing the Eiffel Tower behind a fearful woman who climbed at a pace I could handle without offending those behind me.

After what seemed like forever, I made it to the lower level and did so without passing out. Once there, I took some time to get acquainted with my surroundings and began to seek the Lord's direction. There was a dining area, a restaurant, and tables and chairs for tourists to sit on. Around the perimeter of the first level, there was a walkway enclosed by a fence, so you could see out for miles without the risk of falling.

As I gathered myself, I tuned in to the Lord and felt Him lead me to walk around the perimeter. As I got closer to the spot I was to pray at, I would begin to feel it in my spirit. This is what happened exactly. As I moved down the walkway on the west side of the tower, I began feeling an increased sensation of the Lord's presence. When I got to the corner, I felt the full intensity of the presence of the Lord. As I continued on beyond the corner, I felt the presence diminish, but when I returned to the corner, it came back. I knew this was the spot. I was there ahead of schedule, so I did my best to blend in as a tourist by looking around and listening to some music on my phone.

Rending the Veil

The moment was now at hand for my whole purpose for being on the first level of the Eiffel Tower in Paris, France. What I am about to share was a dramatic, life-altering moment. Before this trip, I had read about angelic encounters, listened to sermons about ministers experiencing the angelic, and read the Scriptures that described the interaction between angels and humans.

All of these, however, were other people's stories and events. What I am sharing is what happened to me, my firsthand account. This was my first interaction with an angel as an adult. God did not lead me in slowly, He tossed me in and pushed my "weird meter" further beyond what I thought I could handle. It changed me, and it set the stage for my future co-laboring with God's precious angels.

As the moment approached for me to release the angel, I saw a veil. It looked like a sheet that separated the physical reality from the spiritual reality. I was standing on the side of it and able to see both realities simultaneously. To my left was the spiritual reality. Immediately in front of the veil was an immense angel. To my right was the physical reality with people sightseeing and milling around the outer walking area.

I felt led to move to my right and face the veil. Leading up to the trip, the Lord had given me a spiritual sword. As I stood in front of this divine curtain, I knew I was to unsheathe the sword. With this knowledge came the understanding that I was to use it to make a cut through the veil to release the angel into our reality. Bear in mind: I was to do this as a prophetic act. I was to put my hand behind my head, remove the sword and make a cut in the veil as an actual physical action. Also, keep in mind that there were scores of people all around me, so looking inconspicuous was going to be a challenge.

As the seconds ticked down to the exact moment, I positioned myself and did my best not to draw attention. I removed the sword from a sheathe that was strapped to my back and lifted the sword out over my head. With the sword drawn, I reached as high as I could and plunged the sword into the veil. I drew the sword down through the curtain with both hands and stopped a foot or so above the ground. I re-sheathed the sword and took a few steps back. What I saw next was one of the most amazing things I have ever seen spiritually in my entire walk as a Christian.

The Angel Steps Through

From where I stood, I could clearly see the cut in the spiritual veil. Then suddenly, I saw the angel put his head through the veil. The veil prohibited me from seeing the angel, so when his head passed through the cut, it was beyond description. Seeing the angel's head poke through the veil was overwhelming, but what happened next left me at a complete loss for words.

The angel's head was protruding through the cut in the veil. Suddenly, the angel lowered his head to the lowest point of the cut in the veil. I was bewildered by this action; I was not at all sure what he was doing. Then the angel's wings began to come through the cut in the veil. It was utterly wondrous to behold.

The angel was tall, and his wings extended 2-3 feet above his head. The slit I cut in the veil was not tall enough for the angel to walk through, so the angel had to lower his entire being to allow his wings to come through. Once the head and wings were through, the first leg came through followed by the other leg. As the angel came through the veil into the natural realm, he stood up straight. He stood close to 20 feet tall when standing fully upright with wings extending above his head.

The night before this assignment, I had a very clear and vivid vision of a large angel. The angel I released was this angel. I noticed that the corner the Lord led me to for this supernatural experience had a higher ceiling than the other three corners of the Eiffel Tower. There was a metal frame that said 20 feet. The fullness of the angel stopped just a few inches short of this sign. Again, I was amazed, astounded, and humbled before my God.

Once the angel stood fully up, he expanded his chest (he was very muscular), rolled his shoulders back, and flexed the muscles of his upper torso. It looked like he was stretching. I was standing next to him on the side of his right leg. I just came up to about his knees.

I stared up at his face, and he looked down at me and winked at me with a slight smile. Then, he shifted his focus toward the west and stared intently becoming utterly motionless. He appeared like he was physically locked into this position. I was no longer aware of the people around me. I wonder how I looked to anyone watching me.

After a few minutes, I heard the Lord speak to me. He said that angels exist to serve Him, and this angel would remain at this location until time ended. I found myself feeling sad for the angel that he would stand watch and be on guard alone.

The Lord spoke to me again and said that the angel was devoted to Him and felt honored to serve Him in this way. The Lord then told me the angel's name and said that when time does end, the angel will find me in Heaven and discuss this assignment with me.

The Best for Last

This was my first trip where angels played an observable role. I saved it for last because of all that transpired. I have seen and encountered numerous angels, but this one prepared me for a life of interacting with everyday angels. Angels are all around us.

Just recently, our 19-month-old child had to have blood drawn. My wife had to restrain her while the nurses approached with needles. I felt utterly helpless as a dad, watching my baby's distress. When I looked up over my wife's left shoulder, an angel was standing there making sure everything went smoothly. Peace quickly arrived.

This is part of your salvation package, too. The Bible says we have not because we ask not. I promise you that all the glorious wonders of God are a simple request away. Start asking and you will start receiving. It is not my promise; it is God's!

My Prayer for You

Father, I pray that every person that reads this will book will be moved and awakened to a new level of who they are in You. I pray that as my brother or sister grows in their ability to see with the eyes of their heart, the invisible real would become visible. Even at this moment, I pray that they would discern the angels that You sent. Teach my brothers and sisters how to co-labor with angels, so their daily lives take on a supernatural quality they never knew existed. I pray they would be overwhelming conquerors in the name of Jesus Christ. Amen.

What About You?

- I shared the story about meeting my French friends and their divinely ordained help in the airport. Can you recall a time when the circumstances you were in could only exist by the hand of God? How did that make you feel? How often do you think things like this should happen?

- After reading these stories about co-laboring with angels, have your ideas about partnering with angels expanded? Have you asked the Lord how He would have you partner with angels yet? What did He tell you?

- Use the "Stroll Along the Sea of Galilee" meditation at www.cwgministries.org/galilee. In two-way journaling, ask: Lord, what angelic assignment would You give to me where I can release Your provision to a people in need? How do You want me to partner with angels?

- Tune into the flow of the Holy Spirit. Look to see what comes. In childlike faith, write down what you see and hear. Ask God to confirm it to you through other means. Trust Him to do that. Act on what you see and release God's provision into places of need.

Chapter 14

Timeless: Living in the Eternal Now of God

by Charity Kayembe

My friend Shannon lives in New Zealand and has crazy angel adventures. He actually gets excited when there is demonic activity, because that means he and his angels get to do some damage to the enemy's kingdom! He likes going to war with his angelic back-up because they fight in God's strength and the victory Jesus already secured. Shannon knows he's on the winning side.

Recently, he shared a revelation with me that he had about time. Shannon began noticing that his angels would go off to fight before he actually dispatched them. Here is his story.

> I wanted to tell you about an experience that happened to me the other day.

I had a single mum call me and ask for help. I told her what God was showing me and this helped her to share the following. She had been having dark thoughts around cutting and suicide. She had not been sleeping well at all, and had her kids waking up throughout the night with demonic apparitions scaring them. I told her what God was telling me about her next moves, and I asked her if it was ok to send angels to her home. She said, "Yes, please."

Anyway, I put the phone down and was immediately distracted by my wife as we were sitting down to watch a movie together. At the end of the movie I was reminded to pray for angels.

As I opened my mouth, Jesus intervened and said to me, "I have already sent the angels you asked for and the number you wanted." Now, I had sent NO angels and had no number in mind. So, I said to the Lord, "500 angels." At the same exact time, He said to me, "500 angels."

I was stunned that as soon as I intended to send the angels they were sent, even though I never followed through by releasing them.

It confirms what I'd been thinking... do angels move outside of time? You betcha!

On another occasion, Shannon heard about a situation at a friend's property and discerned demonic activity was the underlying problem. He told his friend that he couldn't come himself, but he would send angels over to take care of things.

Shannon fully intended to commission some angels; however, as he hung up the phone an angel told him, "Don't worry, we're on our way. In fact, we're already there! We are getting it sorted. You don't worry about it; you focus on your work, and we'll handle it."

This is similar to what Daniel experienced. An angel said, "Do not be afraid, Daniel, for from the first day that **you set your heart** on understanding this and on humbling yourself before your God, your words were heard, and I have come in response to your words." (Dan. 10:12).

The last example I'll share was the time Shannon was about to pray for a girl who needed deliverance. Shannon took a breath and was just about to cast out the enemy, but before he had the chance to utter a word, he saw two huge angels lop the heads off two unclean spirits that were hanging onto the girl.

Before he prayed, it was done. Before we call, He has answered (see Isa. 65:24)!

Supernatural Communication

Does that mean we don't always have to verbally activate and dispatch our angels? No, we don't. However, we still must *intend* to. Shannon did not actually have to commission them; but he did have to think about commissioning them. Once it was his intention, the angels knew what to do and they did it. Again, supernatural communication is spirit to spirit, feeling to feeling, thought to thought (see Mark 2:8).

But Shannon's revelation is about more than that. It is about the fluidity of time and how those in the spirit are not confined by our limited perception of it. My dad once commissioned his angel for a very important, involved assignment. But almost as soon as he had sent him off, the angel was back again. He had left, accomplished the mission, and returned, in what seemed like only a moment!

In this chapter, we will explore the eternal now of God, that outside-of-time dimension in which angels dwell. As you begin interacting with your own angels, you will quickly realize there is neither distance nor time in the spirit realm. Scientifically, this can be explained through the principles of non-locality and the instantaneous nature of quantum entanglement. I have written on how our walk in the Spirit correlates with quantum physics[30] and highly recommend Pastor Phil Mason's book *Quantum Glory: The Science of Heaven Invading Earth* for more on the subject.

For now, we simply want to examine what Scripture has to say about the nature of time, and our relationship to it. Once we understand God's original design, we understand how angels would know we are going to partner with them. Angels can see the "future," because to them it is not the future. It just is. And since they know we *will* partner with them, they are able to do the work that needs to be done even before we ask them, since there is no "before."

Emily Dickinson was right when she said, "Forever is composed of nows."[31] There is only now. There is only ever now. The eternal now of the great I AM (see Ex. 3:14). This realm of timelessness is the dimension in which angels and God live. It is a dimension we are invited to live in, too.

The Persistent Illusion of Time

Jesus said, "I am the Alpha and the Omega, the first and the last, the beginning and the end," which puts Him squarely and decidedly outside of time (see Rev. 22:13). He is timeless, and we're supposed to be just like Him. Even Einstein said, "The distinction between past, present, and future is only a stubbornly persistent illusion."[32]

I used to feel like every other thing about God we should aspire to live into—His holiness, His strength, His love. I understood how all of His attributes could work in our natural world, except for timelessness. Didn't He create this world with time, and then place us inside of it? God is eternal, but didn't He make it so that we don't have everlasting life on this earth, in this world?

God created time. In Genesis, we learn that God declared evening and morning. He also spoke into being the lights in the heavens to separate the day from the night and to mark seasons and days and years (see Gen. 1:13-14). There is no question that He created time and then put us where it is.

Which is why, of all the spiritual revelations in quantum physics I wanted to experience, the one thing I had been most challenged with was the dimension of time. I realized that it only appears linear, but how could we ever transcend it? Since God created time, I wasn't sure how to live outside of it or if we should even try to do so.

I used to be extraordinarily aware of time, and I always felt I had too little of it. I lived in a constant state of rush, thinking about getting on to the next thing on my to-do list. I once managed to get three speeding tickets in just one year! I knew time well, and it would bear down on me at every turn.

The Revelation

So let's re-visit the original question: Did God create time in this world, and put us inside of it? Yes, He created time. But no, He did not put us in time, as in, under the constraints of it. We did that to ourselves.

God made seasons and time and hours and days, but He also created us to be eternal. To live forever (see Gen. 3:22). There was no death before sin. And without death, time becomes irrelevant, or at least fairly inconsequential.

Even though there was time before The Fall, there was no end to it. With no end to time, it's as if it didn't exist. We were never meant to live under the restrictions of time. One result of the curse was to come under the oppression of time, to experience death, and to see the world start passing away. But this was not God's original intention or design.

Serving Time

How do we tend to view time? Rather violently it turns out. For example, we talk about killing time, being pressed for time, and being in a time crunch. We even talk about *deadlines*!

I don't want to be pressed, crunched, or dead!

Of course, I'm not suggesting we should stop using our watches or clocks. There is a time that a flight is scheduled to depart, and it's best if I show up at the designated time and terminal. For now, it is convenient to simply arrange a place and time to meet a friend for lunch. So yes, I do use time for that. I use time, though; it is not the boss of me.

We intuitively know that time shouldn't govern us, because when someone is in prison, we say they are "serving time." We recognize we are not to serve time. Time is to serve us. Just like Jesus said, the Sabbath was created for man; not man for the Sabbath (see Mark 2:27). So, too, time was created for man, to serve and bless us—not to reign over us. God wants to give back to us the reins of time, so we are no longer serving two masters.

In the Garden of Eden, time was not their god. God was their God. But for me, I was so often tempted to be a slave of time, to let it be my taskmaster. I used to mistakenly assume that if I am to be a good steward of the limited amount of time I have on the earth, I should hurry up and accomplish lots of ministry work and worthwhile goals.

Jesus and Time

However, let's consider Jesus. He had some huge responsibilities, what with redeeming fallen humanity and saving the world. He had less time here on earth than I've already had, but even with His ambitious mission, He still found time to live. He got alone with Father. He played with children. He slept. With all there was to do in the world, He still had the perspective that #1—He wasn't supposed to do everything, and #2—He didn't let time rule His life.

Somehow, being in a hurry diminishes us. Kings and priests are never in a hurry. If they were in a hurry, we would be tempted to think they were an imposter. To allow myself to be pressured by time diminishes almost everything about me, my work, and even my great intentions.

So I decided I did not want time to rule my life. I did not want time to drive me like a rancher drives his cattle with force and pressure. But since time is a part of the world I'm living in, I purposed to use it as it suits me best. It can still drive me, but in a different way.

I had a dream that encouraged me that I was successfully living into this new revelation. The dream was about time, and I was being driven by a chauffeur. So yes, time can drive me—but as my servant. Because God is outside of time, and we are His children created in His image, we are not beneath time or under its control either. It is His intention for us to live above and beyond time's limits and restrictions. "As He is, so also are we in this world" (1 John 4:17).

We see demonstrations of this throughout Scripture and know these things were written as examples for us. Philip was translated, changing locations outside of the confines of time and how long it should take to get somewhere (see Acts 8:39-40). Jesus saw all the kingdoms of the world in a moment in time (see Luke 4:5). God massaged Elijah's relationship with time when he outran the chariot (see 1 Kings 18:46). The shadow moved backward 10 steps for Hezekiah, and the sun stood still for Joshua (see 2 Kings 20:8-11; Josh. 10:12-13).

Edge of Time

When I was growing up, we rented a farmhouse. All around the farm were fields, and the fields were surrounded by barbed wire fences. I picture that there is a fence of time around the physical world, but whenever God wants, He can lift up that fence wire. We can slip right underneath it and into a timeless dimension, experiencing all manner of extraordinary things.

Then when we're done, we slide back under that fence of time and are basically right where we started. Like Narnia. The Pevensie children grew up and lived an entire life on the other side of the wardrobe, and when they came back it had just been an afternoon. "With the Lord one day is as a thousand years, and a thousand years is as one day" (2 Pet. 3:8). God is I AM—not I was or I will be—so we want to be present and live into His eternal now.

What does that look like in real life? If we don't worship time, does that mean we should just mosey and meander as slow as molasses through our days? Do we not pay attention to time at all and take forever to get things done or to get to places?

Hardly. While I know this revelation of time has changed absolutely everything for me, it has also changed almost nothing at all. More than anything, it's an internal shift in how I see time and relate to it. Just like my parents teach in *How to Walk by the Spirit*,[33] my underlying attitudes and motivations about time have changed. What is the spirit level reason for my doing whatever I'm doing?

Fast or Furious

There is an important distinction here that I don't want you to miss. We can still move swiftly and efficiently through our day and our lives, even perhaps as "fast" as before. The difference on the outside can be quite subtle. It's a change on the inside that allows us to move quickly, but from a place of inner peace and strength and grace.

Fast is fine. Speed is fine. There is a big difference, though, between being fast and being in a hurry. They are not the same thing. It is the difference between moving quickly and being rushed. It is the heart and spirit motivation that is at issue, not so much the outward actions.

Hurried, rushed, pressured—those are all underlying feelings, thoughts and motivations that are causing the speedy behavior. There's nothing wrong with speed, unless it is motivated by a hurried spirit.

What is ever better when it's done in a hurry? Nothing I can think of. At first I thought maybe race car drivers or competitive athletes; those races should be done in a hurry. But no. Again, those races are done quickly and with speed. They race fast, but if they're good at what they do and actually win their competitions, those racers are not in a place of panic, rush or stress. They need to be centered down and acting from a place of calm and inner peace if they're going to not crash their cars at 200 mph.

There is a place for adrenaline. It's all well and good as long as it's not pumping through our systems several times a day for no reason other than we're running a few minutes late. That's just not how God designed our bodies to live and run optimally.

Nature is an even better example. Consider a cheetah—the fastest animal God made. A cheetah moves quickly but gracefully. He runs fast because he wants to. He's powerful and intentional. Fast, but not hurried. Quick, but not rushed. We can be like the cheetah.

We just don't want to be like a chicken, running around with its head cut off! Sure he's moving fast too, but the motivation is totally different. He's afraid and moving out of compulsion. Although he's moving fast, he's really not going anywhere, running around in circles, worried about dying. And really, isn't that what we are ultimately worried about if we worry about time? What are we going to be able to squeeze in and accomplish and have and be and do before we die?

Vision of a Trap

We need to maintain a timeless perspective in a world that is controlled by time. It's important to learn how to protect our spirits from becoming hurried, which can release the stress hormone cortisol into our body. The goal is to keep *Jesus* as Lord of our lives and not become a servant to time.

I had a vision of a cage that was trying to trap me. It was big and metal and cold and hard and it came down toward me at an angle, trying to cover me and keep me inside. The cage was Time, and it attempted to confine and press me into lockdown from all sides, gripping, controlling and enslaving me.

I realized though if I looked at it, intentionally observed it for what it was—a trap—that would stop it in its tracks and it wouldn't be able to come down over me. God was showing me that if I could see time the way He sees it, then I won't be confined or rushed or trapped by it.

Seeing the trap was the key to stopping it, and that was confirmed in the word I kept feeling, which was "seer". I need to be a seer, and that will help me escape the trap and live free and timeless.

Except the word that I saw was "sear," not "seer." What's a "sear"? I didn't know, so I checked an online dictionary and found that one of the definitions for "sear" is a part of a gun.

A Seer or a Sear

A gun? I didn't know anything about guns so I asked my colleague about it. He told me that the sear's job is to prevent the hammer from moving forward when it's not supposed to, which in turn prevents the gun from firing when it shouldn't. If the sear does its job, the bullet remains stationary and there are no accidental explosions.

The revelation dawned: If I do my job as a seer and observe the vision of time God gave me and see things from His point of view, I won't move forward—hurry and rush—when I am not supposed to. A heavenly perspective of time will keep me from "going off" and exploding with stress and pressure.

And you know what? That has actually worked really well! As entirely subjective as this exercise appears to be, it is confirmed by Phil Mason's extensive research. With regards to British physicist Paul Davies, Mason writes, "Davies is perhaps one of the world's leading authorities on time and its relationship to space, and he has concluded that time is a product of the observer rather than an objective attribute of space, as Einstein's theory of general relativity also suggests."[34]

Wow! No wonder that just by altering my perception of time, I have become so much more peaceful and relaxed. I am no longer stressed out all the time. I feel rest as a state of being.

Retroactive Prayer

Once we begin living to the truth that time is not a rationed commodity in short supply, we won't worry about running out of it. We realize that our supernatural prayers transcend time. God and His angels work outside of any boundaries or barriers of time that our narrow perception artificially creates.

An extraordinary testimony of how this works and what it potentially means for us is cited by Dawson Church, Ph.D.:

> Another example of the power of prayer across time comes
> from a study published in the British Medical Journal in
> 2001. In Israel, Professor Leonard Leibovici took a stack

of hospital case histories and divided it into two random piles. The patients in these cases had all been admitted for blood poisoning. Names in one stack were prayed for, while the others were not.

On later analysis, the group prayed for was found to have a reduced rate of fevers, shorter hospital stays, and a lower mortality rate. This kind of finding is typical of prayer studies and would not have surprised most researchers— except that the patients Leibovici prayed for had been discharged from hospital ten years earlier. The healing power of consciousness and intention appears to be independent of time as well as space. Prayer seems to work retroactively, as well as across great distances.[35]

God knew those patients would be prayed for. Our prayers go into the spirit realm where there is no time or distance. Father honored the prayer offered in the "future" and healing was released in the "past." The more we learn to see time the way God sees time, the more confidently we can live in a comfortable relationship with it. We will see time as something we can step into and out of and even move around, because time is fluid and flexible.

Angels know this. That is how they live. The more we interact with them, the more we will understand that their perspective of time is different from ours. There is no hurry, there is no rush, there is no late.

There just IS.

It is the eternal now of God, and He has placed that eternity in our hearts (see Eccl. 3:11). As God's children, created in His image, and indeed members of His very own Body, we are not constricted, confined, or constrained by time either. Time was only ever intended to bless us, designed as a generous gift from our loving heavenly Father.

An Excuse for Sunsets

It does beg the question, though, why did God invent time if not to constrain us?

While there may be many answers to this question, my current personal favorite is sunsets.

What is time? What makes it up? Days, seasons, years. Well, seasons are lovely! Who doesn't admire colorful fall leaves and new spring bulbs and all the rhythms of nature? Indeed, there is no better way to start each morning than with a bright and beautiful sunrise.

Could it be, at least in part, that that is what time was originally about? For our pleasure? God so delighted in our company, relaxing in the Garden in the cool of the day with us, He decided time would be an ideal reason to paint the sky. With varying shades of brilliance He splashes His glory across the canvas of heaven, giving us something to anticipate and enjoy as we stroll along with Him sharing life together.

So maybe...just maybe...time was an excuse for sunsets.

What About You?

- How have you tended to view time? After reading this chapter, has your perspective changed at all? In what way?

- In chapter 12, you learned several different ways to get "in spirit." What have you tried so far, and which ways have been most helpful?

- Use your favorite approach to quiet down into your heart. Imagine Jesus and your angels with you, then ask Holy Spirit to enlighten your spiritual eyes and transform that picture into His vision. Tune to flow and write down the spontaneous thoughts you receive back from the following questions.

- Lord, what would You like to speak to me about time? Am I viewing it the way You want me to view it? What are Your thoughts about time?

- You can also ask your angels if they have anything they'd like to share with you about the eternal dimension in which they dwell. How do they see time?

  When I asked my angels this question, Shobis began in a mock serious tone quoting, "Time waits for no man..."

  Pojes finished his thought for him laughing, "...good thing we're not men! Ha!"

  They never cease to amuse themselves or me with their crazy antics. Apparently, almost everything is fun when you are an angel.

  And as they have pointed out, they are in Heaven—so why wouldn't it be fun?

Chapter 15

Testimonies from Around the World

by Charity Kayembe

Angels are on the move, and it's always so exciting to hear what they are up to in other corners of the globe. Throughout this book, Joe and I have shared our stories, but we are by no means the only ones interacting with angels. I trust you will be inspired by these powerful testimonies confirming that the angelic realm is for everyone, and that includes you!

The Angel in My Dream

I met Pastor Duncan and Rachel Jeffery when I had the privilege of teaching on dream interpretation at their fellowship, Te Puke Baptist Church, in Northern New Zealand. Eden is their lovely 13-year-old daughter who is good friends with her guardian angel. Here is her testimony, in her own words.[36]

Hi, here's my angel story...

I met my angel in a dream. This is what happened in my dream... I was going through this big tunnel and there were lots of people saying "Turn right Eden, turn right."

So, I turned right. I kept on going for a little while and then I saw a big bright light. It was so bright I had to shut my eyes. I kept walking slowly shutting my eyes tighter. Then I heard a voice saying, "Open your eyes, Eden," so I did. I opened my eyes. I saw my angel. He was wonderful. I could not take my eyes off him.

I studied him. He was huge, about twice as tall as me (I'm 153 cm or 5' tall). Super shiny, sparkly (so shiny he was hard to look at). White robe. Every time he moved, the robe swayed around like silk. He had something white on his head (maybe a halo or feather crown).

Bare feet—they were perfect feet. Soft, quiet, gentle feet. He was so bright, I could barely look at him. Indescribable! I knew he was my angel. His name is Ian. I talk to him often. I met him 4 years ago (29 June 2013), I was 9 years old then.

I love that she was first introduced to her angel in a dream. Yes, dreams are bridges to the supernatural! And my favorite part of her description is of the feet: quiet, gentle, perfect feet. How beautiful are the feet of those who bring good news!

Outback Angels

It was a pleasure getting to know Rebecca and Emily Calvert's family in New South Wales, Australia. They are the worship leaders at the church their parents pastor, and we had some awesome workshops together on the sacred supernatural.

My husband and I fell in love with their whole family and found we had much in common, including seeing angels. I have asked both of these amazing women of God to share a few of their stories with us.

Angel of Joy by Rebecca Calvert

When Charity was teaching on angels and told us to ask God if we had angels, He told me I have 12 around me at various times. Josiah is the main guy. I have also met Samuel, Joy, and Jabbok.

One of my earlier angelic encounters was when I was around 12, and we had taken a car trip to Canberra for a day out. I had taken a travel sickness tablet and the side effect was drowsiness. We went on a pushbike ride around a lake. I was a bit out of it, as the drugs were still working, and at the end of the ride I rode straight towards four lanes of traffic instead of into the carpark.

My parents could see what was happening, but they were too far behind to catch me. Before I went onto the road, someone appeared and pulled me back to safety. Mum caught up to me, and when they looked up the stranger had totally disappeared. I believe that was my angel, too.

I often see angels but one other experience especially stands out for me. As long as I can remember, I have picked up a little on what's happening in the atmosphere around me, good and bad. (While at university, I used to sleep in my wardrobe when the world felt unsafe. Many nights I just didn't sleep.)

I was living in Sydney, about 4 ½ hours away from my country hometown. One night I woke up around midnight and knew there was a large looming demon at the end of my bed. I was freaked out. Then I remembered that God is bigger. So I cried out, literally cried.... told the demon to go and asked for protection. I asked God for long-term protection through the rest of my life, so I could feel safe (and sleep). The demon vanished and Holy Spirit stepped in.

He showed me two VERY large angels on either side of my bed. Josiah was to my left. He has stayed with me ever since.

Then I saw a very little angel, like super small. I asked God what he was doing, as he was way too small to protect me. God said, "He's actually the best protection you have. His name is Joy, and although he's small he actually provides the most protection out of your three."

Joy looks like an old school angel in the white/gold robe and has a trumpet, but without wings. He's funny and laughs so much! Every time I see or think about him, he's somewhere around my head. He told me he protects my thoughts and blows joy right into my brain!

Amen! God told her that Joy is her strongest protection, and we know Scripture says the joy of the Lord strengthens us (see Neh. 8:10). What is most fascinating about Rebecca's guardians is that her biggest protector was the smallest angel. I love that, and I have found a similar principle to be true in my walk in the spirit. Some things are opposite of how they appear in the material world.

For example, in the natural realm we only see our physical bodies with our physical eyes. Our hearts and spirits are hidden inside and are essentially invisible. This is reversed in the supernatural realm at times. Man looks on the outward appearance, but angels are like God in that they look on the heart (see 1 Sam. 16:7). More than our flesh and blood, they see our anger or our love. They see our fear or our joy. Paul said we should know no one according to the flesh (see 2 Cor. 5:16). Angels do not know us according to the flesh. They sense our spirits first and foremost, and that is predominantly what they see.

Bumping Into an Angel by Emily Calvert

Three friends and I decided to have a New Year's adventure last December. None of us are hikers, or even regular campers, and we definitely know nothing about mountains. Despite that, we all borrowed rucksacks, packed too many kilos of gear, and laced up our new hiking boots. We set off to climb Australia's seven highest peaks (the highest is only 2228 meters), on a stormy morning, in the rain!

We took our boots off for two small creek crossings and started toward our first peak. By the time we had reached the summit we decided to skip the next, farther peak and continue on to find somewhere to set up camp, as the wind was blowing so strongly against us that we were walking two-by-two to hold each other up!

The rain was biting and cold, and we didn't stay waterproof for long. We found out later that the wind gusts were up to 85km per hour, though it felt even faster standing on the ridge! It took us 3 hours to get over the top, another hour to set the tent up—by which time the other three had mild hypothermia. I was quite worried, but we were all clueless and pushed on.

An hour later, we all had dry clothes on and had made hot food. Then we prayed. The rain hadn't let up, and we were holding up the tent by pushing our rucksacks against the wall the wind was pushing on, and then leaning up against the bags.

We asked God what to do, and as soon as we finished asking, my sister, the most sensitive listener in our group, burst into tears and wanted to go back. So back down we went! The tent was rolled up quickly, and just as quickly we all got drenched! The rain was heavy and horizontal, falling in stunning waves on the mountain slopes.

We had to hike back up to the peak, and as we plodded upward, heads down, I met an angel. I hardly ever see angels, even when I'm looking! But I was aware that God was leading us and protecting us. And then it was almost like I bumped into this big, burly angel.

I asked his name. It was Azariah. I asked him what he was doing there, and he said he'd been sent to buoy our spirits. By this time, we were on the descent, and so much water was rushing down the path that we were walking in a shallow stream!

It should have been scary, or at the least, miserable. But both my sister and I had incredible encounters and revelations from God on our walk back, we were delighted to be in the midst of the beautiful storm, and we knew we were safe.

I did ask Azariah if he could not only buoy my spirits but also lift some of the weight from my soaked rucksack, and he just chuckled. It was such a bizarre experience: first (intended) overnight hike, first almost-hypothermia, first time being in the middle of such a wild, gloriously unrestrained storm.

In an hour, we reached the creek crossings. Leaving our boots on we sent the tallest two in our group across. The water had been at mid-calf height when we crossed earlier, and now it was lapping at our hips. Our strongest friend came back for the shortest in our group and took her bag, as she was in up to her waist.

At that point, I was amused that God had used the word 'buoy,' as I confidently put the shortest girl between us and crossed for the last ascent to the car. We had lasted only 6 hours of our 3-day hike.

We did go back up the next day from another point though. The sky was clear blue and the sun was so hot we all got burned! We spent New Year's Eve camped in the shadow of our highest peak, but I knew from the day before, that we were sheltered in the shadow of the Almighty.

A few days later, on January 3rd, God told me to read Daniel. There, in 1:6 was Azariah! His name means "God has helped." What awesome confirmation!

Teaching "Assistance"

My father and I have both had participants at various workshops tell us they see angels with us while we are teaching. This is always encouraging to hear!

Sometimes people see the angels standing next to us or behind us. This past weekend, a lady saw two huge angels on each end of the platform Dad was standing on. She said she saw them watching over the words he was speaking to ensure they were not stolen but heard correctly in the hearts of those present.

I love that revelation, as it is such a beautiful illustration of one more way we may partner together with the angelic realm in serving our King.

Angel Rescue

Ray Fisher has been a wonderful friend of our family for many, many years. I first heard this harrowing angel rescue story when I was a little girl, and I have never forgotten it. I know you will be equally impacted by the dramatic testimony so I asked him to share it with you here.

> I have been protected from a lot of crazy things over the years. One of the most significant happened even before I was a Christian, back in 1974 when I was 31 years old. I had a boating accident when I was fishing with my girlfriend's brother, Randy. We were near Wilmington, North Carolina and a Nor'easter was heading in. We knew spot fish came then, and we could make some good money, so we grabbed our beer and fishing nets and took our chances with the storm.
>
> It turned bad quickly and we haphazardly drew the nets and threw them on the bow of the boat. Once we started moving, though, the nets fell off and became tangled in the motor. This caused the boat to turn so sharply to the left that Randy and I were both thrown overboard into the ocean.
>
> I was okay but Randy was tangled in the net, so I went to help him. I managed to free him, but in the process became entangled myself. I was under water, and I couldn't get free. The boat kept circling overhead. It circled around 10 times. By that point, I was so exhausted from the struggle that I knew I was going to die.
>
> The eleventh time the boat passed by, it caught me, and the 115 horsepower Mercury outboard motor tore through

the brachial artery of my right arm. I actually saw fish nibbling on my flesh, but I didn't feel a thing. I somehow managed to swim to shore and drag myself up onto the beach. Blood was gushing everywhere, and I still knew I was going to die.

All I could remember to pray was, "The Lord is my shepherd. The Lord is my shepherd," over and over again. As I did, the Heavens were opened and I saw behind the veil into the spirit realm. There were angels battling over me. Angels with armor of light were protecting me from the onslaught of angels with armor of darkness.

The next thing I knew I was being transported to the hospital. After several months, I eventually recovered, which was a miracle nobody expected. I still even have use of my right hand! I ended up coming to Christ three years to the day after this boating accident.

After I got saved, I eventually asked the Lord about that day and where He was during my accident. I knew that angels were with me on the beach, but where were they when I was trapped underwater and under the boat? Why weren't they protecting me from getting my forearm shredded by the motor?

Immediately, I had a supernatural flashback to the scene, and saw what actually happened, from God's perspective. I saw myself desperately flailing. My body was floating upward toward the surface of the water and directly into the path of the motor.

I realized that just at that moment, an angel shoved me downward, deeper under the water, to prevent my head from colliding with the motor. My arm was still floating higher in the water above my head, so it did get struck. However, if the angel had not pushed me down deeper and out of the way, then it would have been my head which struck the motor. Of course, that would have been fatal.

I knew I was much deeper under the surface of the water than I should have naturally been. I just never realized why. At that moment, I received an even greater revelation of God's heart and His love, and how He has faithfully protected me my whole life. Even before I was living for Him, He had His angels watching out for me and fighting for me.

There are so many lessons we can take away from this powerful testimony. Even before we believe in Jesus, He believes in us. Not one of us has ever been alone. Not one of us has ever been unloved. And sometimes what we see as the "worst of times" really isn't as bad as it could be. We always have Someone watching over us, and we always, always have something to be grateful for.

Surrounded by Angels

"Do not fear, for those who are with us are more than those who are with them!" Then Elisha prayed, "O Lord, open his eyes that he may see." And the Lord opened the young man's eyes and he saw: the mountain was full of horses and chariots of fire all around Elisha. (2 Kings 6:16-17)

It is always such a blessing to receive testimonies of God's supernatural realm breaking into our world through dreams and angels, and this next story is another favorite because it involves both!

Heaven's Cheerleaders *by Karen*

Hi Charity, I want to tell you how profoundly your *Hearing God Through Your Dreams* teaching and book have touched me. I was at Invercargill Christian Centre to hear your night service message. Our pastor at the daughter church, Winton CC, had encouraged us to go and, full of skepticism, I was obedient to what I knew was as close to a command as Pastor Stephen was going to give.

The words you spoke resonated and embedded themselves deep inside me. I bought your book and that very first night instructed my heart to be ready to hear from God... and I did! Since then I have had dreams nearly every night, and they have helped us through a huge challenge in our marriage as well as in countless other personal situations.

The most powerful dream, however, I believe will have an impact on our family for generations to come. It is about our little granddaughter who, at five years old, puts huge pressure on herself to learn and excel. She has found school increasingly challenging and becomes distressed that she may not be able to learn well enough.

God showed me in a dream that when she started to feel fearful and wanted to cry, she should shut her eyes and look inside herself. She would see that God had surrounded her with angels all encouraging her on, clapping and cheering at what she was doing. I told my daughter about the dream and at the end of vacation time, when Sarah was getting worked up about returning to school, my daughter Ruth told her the dream I had for her.

The next day, when Sarah got home from school, her dad asked her how the day went.

Sarah replied, "It was great. When I got upset and wanted to cry, I just shut my eyes and looked inside myself. I saw my angels and knew it was all right, so I just carried on with my work. I didn't even cry."

Then Sarah trotted off to play.

God ministered to me, and then tangibly to the next two generations, providing a vital key to dealing with Sarah's fears, which had been concerning all of us. The far-reaching result of hearing one message at church stuns me, as does my gratitude for the new world that God has opened.

Now, when I have a night without a dream, I feel a bit like my best friend has gone on holiday, and I can't wait to reconnect. Thank you, Charity, for your ministry and your work. My life is changed and stepped up to a whole new level. Bless you!

What Took You So Long?

I was talking with my friend Kristie about our angelic bodyguards. She could sense her angels but didn't know she could ask them their names. My testimony encouraged her, so she asked and learned both of their names. I was very happy to hear that, and also that she didn't keep the revelation to herself.

I have a friend at church who senses his angels as well, so I asked if he knew his angels' names. He didn't, so I suggested he ask them. He wasn't sure we should actually do that, so I told him that you know the angels are there, and that they're under God's authority. So if you ask and you're not supposed to know, then they just won't answer you.

That made sense to him and he tried it. Not only did both angels tell him their names and introduce themselves, they said, "Why didn't you ask us sooner?"

I love it! I had shared my testimony with Kristie, which encouraged her to interact with her angels. Kristie shared her testimony with a friend, which encouraged him to interact with his angels. The ripple effect of our testimonies is powerful and exponential (see Rev. 12:11).

Better Than AAA

My mom Patti has a beautiful testimony of a "stranger appearing from nowhere" at just the right moment to help her in a time of need, which enabled her to reach my dad and brother safely.

> Josh and Mark had gone snowmobiling together, and one of their machines broke down about an hour from home. They made it to a restaurant and called me to bring the trailer to pick them up. Unfortunately, the trailer was not hooked up to the truck, and I had no idea how to do it.
>
> Frantically praying, I made the connections as well as I could and started out. By the time I got to the gas station less than a mile away, I knew it was never going to make it all the way to them. I pulled into the station and parked along the edge, away from the pumps, and got out to see if there was anything I could do.
>
> I still couldn't figure it out, so I looked around to see if anyone could help me. There were no cars at the pumps and only a young girl at the register who didn't know any more than I did. I walked back to the truck, upset and near tears. I was standing there helplessly looking at the wires and the trailer hitch. I knew I couldn't drive it the

way it was, but I had no way to contact the guys to let them know I couldn't come get them. (This was in the days before cell phones!)

Suddenly, a voice said, "Do you need some help?" I looked up to see a man standing by the trailer and a car parked by the pump not 10 feet from me. I had not heard or seen it pull up, and there really was no way I could have missed it driving so close to me. I said, "Yes, please!" and he quickly made all the connections so I could safely continue. As I drove away, all I could do was thank God for sending an angel to help me.

Entertaining Angels

I had the privilege of teaching at University of the Nations YWAM base in Kona, Hawaii recently where we were blessed with amazing hosts. Sarah and Kevin are ministers from New York who both see angels, as do their teenage children. They agree that they usually appear transparent and they are also quite playful!

I loved when Sarah shared that she saw an angel dancing on top of a palm tree one day. He was laughing and singing about how the palm tree gives glory to God, and how he gives glory to God, too!

As she said that, I looked and could see him. If it is possible to dance the hula and moonwalk at the same time—that angel was doing it. Right on top of a palm tree!

I happily wondered in my heart why he chose the hula... and he just winked at me quipping, "When in Rome...!"

Oh my, what a sight. He was having a ball worshiping God, and we were having a ball being entertained by him. Gives a whole new meaning to the phrase "entertaining angels," that's for sure!

Even indoors, the angels are still quite creative in their high praise to God. During worship Sarah has seen them up near the church roof, swooping in and out of the ceiling fans, having a great time. People often say that angels are attracted to places that are worshipful and joyful, and they bring both of these Kingdom characteristics with them as well. In God's presence is fullness of joy, and the angels are always in God's presence (see Luke 1:19). No wonder it's a non-stop party when they are around!

Supremely Fun

New York Times best-selling author Dr. Marie Chapian has written one of my favorite books on angels, which even includes researched accounts of the angelic throughout Church history. Dr. Chapian has a vibrant conversational relationship with Jesus as well as her angels, and she too testifies to the fun and friendly nature of our heavenly guardians.

> I wish I could express to you how much fun God's angels can be. We tend to think of angels as supremely serious beings wearing supremely serious robes and speaking in supremely serious tones that knock our socks off and make us feel supremely serious.
>
> I have seen angels playing merrily, laughing, and even tickling each other. I've seen angels dancing, cavorting, hopping around, playing, and having fun. I pray with all my heart that you discover the same sense of fun and delight in knowing the Lord and His angels.[37]

The Porch Swing

Likewise, Bobby Connor shares a testimony in his book about the "Angel Cabin" he visited in Moravian Falls, North Carolina. He arrived to a welcome party in the spirit!

"What took you so long?" the angels asked me. As it turned out, they had been stationed there by the Moravians years before and had been without commission for many years. They were very excited I had come, and their jubilation was contagious.

I enjoyed being with them as they swung on the porch swing and then leapt from the porch over eight feet and back without effort. Their joy and gladness felt warm and wonderful. We were having a great time.[38]

I trust you have noticed some remarkable similarities in these testimonies which confirm we are all seeing the same thing: the company of Heaven. In fact, Kevin Basconi has written extensively on angels, and he consistently highlights their unexpected propensity for playfulness.

Smiling, dancing, laughing, winking. It's easy to understand why angels are in such a good mood and always such great company. I imagine it's what we would be like if we were still living in the Garden of Eden, where we wouldn't have any hurt or pain, where we wouldn't be tired or impatient or afraid or overwhelmed, where we wouldn't have experienced sin or its destruction, where everything is perfect.

That is how angels live. They live in Heaven, where it is perfect (see Matt. 18:10). They have never felt the negative effects of a sin nature in their body or mind or heart. They live in a Kingdom of love with a culture of honor. No wonder they are so happy!

Walking with the Wise

When we spend time with angels, we begin to see the world through a more heavenly perspective and eternal point of view. Angels highlight the positives and showcase Father's faithfulness in every situation.

No matter the circumstance, they point us back to Jesus, and He isn't stressed out. Psalm 2:4 tells us that the Lord sits in Heaven and laughs!

We can learn to live the way Jesus and His angels live: peaceful and joyful, loving and compassionate, happy and blessed. The best way to learn to live like them is by learning to live with them. Becoming aware of their presence, spending time with them, interacting with them.

As you practice engaging the supernatural, the easier it will become for you. The mature, through practice, have their senses trained to discern (see Heb. 5:14). The more you look, the more you'll see and the more you listen, the more you'll hear.

The testimony of Jesus is the spirit of prophecy, and God absolutely wants to do for you what He did through His angels for all these people (see Rev. 19:10). I hope you are encouraged more than ever to press into the exciting realms of the spirit. As you continue to journey into the sacred supernatural, soon your life will become full of amazing angel adventures of your own!

What About You?

- Have you said "Good morning" to your angels today? Or smiled in their direction, acknowledging their presence and service to our King?

- Do you have any stories of angelic interaction yet? What was your experience?

- Read Acts chapter 10. Was Cornelius a Christian believer? Was he a Jew? What happened as a result of his obedience to the angel's message?

- Prayerfully meditate on Psalm 16:11. Using your favorite go-to heart tool, quiet yourself down and get "in spirit." Imagine the company of Heaven with you and ask Holy Spirit to breathe on that picture and transform it into His vision. Tune to flowing thoughts and pictures, and in two-way journaling record the answers you receive to these questions.

- Father God, what do You want me to know about joy? What does it mean for Your joy to be my strength?

- How can I remain continually aware of Your presence in order to stay in that place of joy and peace?

- Check in with your angels, too: They live in a Kingdom of joy and peace and love, so what is their perspective on these holy Kingdom emotions?

Chapter 16

Final Thoughts

by Joe Brock

I want to thank you for taking the time to read our book. I feel favored by God to be able to write this with Charity and the Virkler family—they are precious people. As I got to the end of each chapter I penned, I found my mind wandering to you. Yes, you.

I know that I will never meet the majority of the people who will read this book. The truth is that you are important to me because we are family. I want you to know God's grace and love so profoundly; there is nothing in the world that can draw you from Christ's smile. You see, as a team, your success is my success, and my success is yours. This book and the others I hope to write come with a desire to do my part in the years God has given me. I long to inspire all who call Jesus their Lord to fall deeper and deeper in love with Him. I may not know you, but I do know a couple of things about you.

A few years ago, I led my church through Mark Virkler's *Hearing God's Voice* DVD series. Since I arrived at the church I pastor, I talk as often as I can about the beauty and need to hear God, every day, all day. Our spiritual vitality is directly linked to the accepted flow of God's voice in and through our lives. The more we hear and obey, the more supernatural our lives become.

After we finished Mark's DVD series, we met to discuss what we had learned. I arrived at the church an hour or so before the meeting and got things ready. As I was straightening up the chairs, I was chatting with the Lord. I told Him how thrilled I was that this group of people had confirmed journal entries that proved they were all hearing God. I was genuinely happy and excited for them.

Like He so frequently does, God invaded my thoughts and spoke to me. He said something that showed me His heart and tweaked my perception of just how amazing He is. His response was, "Joe, I am happy for them, too, but I am happier for Me. You see, for all their lives I have longed to speak to them. Now that they can hear Me, I get to tell them the things I have always wanted to share, like how I feel about them." All I could do in response was smile. God is good.

Over the last 25 years, after everything I have discovered about God, I am most taken by how He feels about us. Our Father loves us, and if you give Him the freedom to share His heart with you, He will tell you He likes you, too. I have never felt more loved and accepted than I have by God.

This is why this book was written—to inspire you to get to know the God who saved you and to know the full benefits package that came with our salvation. We are not just mere mortals of flesh and blood; we are indeed new creatures in Christ (see 2 Cor. 5:17). The word creature here is the word κτίσις. (pronounced ktis-is). This word connotes a new creation or a new species. Here is what I have concluded about this.

In Genesis 2:7, God exhaled the breath of life into the nostrils of the human form He designed. It is interesting to me that our first breath was an inhale. For me to live, I must first receive.

> *When therefore it was evening, on that day, the first day*
> *of the week, and when the doors were shut where the disci-*
> *ples were, for fear of the Jews, Jesus came and stood in their*
> *midst, and said to them, "Peace be with you." And when*
> *He had said this, He showed them both His hands and His*
> *side. The disciples, therefore, rejoiced when they saw the*
> *Lord. Jesus, therefore, said to them again, "Peace be with*
> *you; as the Father has sent Me, I also send you." And when*
> *He had said this, He breathed on them, and said to them,*
> *"Receive the Holy Spirit.* (John 20:19-22)

Jesus entered a small room somewhere in Jerusalem where the disciples were hiding from the Jews. He invoked peace over them and proved to the group that it was indeed Him. After He spoke peace over them again, He did the unexpected—He breathed on them.

Thousands of years earlier in a garden, God brought forth perfect life through His breath. Here in this room, with this group of men that would change the world, He created a new creature, and like the first time, it was through His breath. At this moment, a new species that hadn't existed before came into existence, a species that could live simultaneously in two realities, the physical and the spiritual. This was a species that carried the infused nature of God in its very being. No species on earth prior to this moment was like this. Our first creation gave us life; our second creation gave us divine life in abundance.

Angels are part of our spiritual reality. The good news is that you received divine breath when you were saved into heavenly places. Just as much as a tree is a part of the physical world you were born into, the angelic is a part of the spiritual world you were also born into.

God helped me understand this concept. With this new understanding came an adjustment about what I thought I had permission to see and experience. Angels are here to help and minister to us and to aid in fulfilling God's divine plan for each of our lives. Without the involvement of angels, I do not believe we can accomplish all God has prepared for us.

I say this because the Bible shows us that God used angels in the unfolding of His plans. If we are to follow the Bible as our example, then angels will be involved in our lives. I am convinced that God desires that we see and work alongside angels every day.

I hope that from what you have read, you are stirred and inspired. I hope you find yourself hungering for more of God and more of what He has given you through your salvation. Because we are a team, I want you to see the angels God has assigned to you and for you to be awakened to their involvement and how God desires that they help you in your everyday life.

Each time my children go somewhere—a ball game, a friend's house, or the mall—I assign angels to them for their protection. I have angels assigned to me, and they are waiting until I give them directions.

You have angels, too! Your angels are waiting for you to co-labor with them. This is God's design, so please do not refuse Him. And remember what Hebrews 1:14 says:

> *Are they not all ministering spirits sent out to serve for the sake of those who are to inherit salvation?*

If you are a reconciled follower of Jesus, you can accept this verse was written for you. The angels are always there; they just need you to involve them in the unfolding of your walk with Jesus. Learn how to partner with them and your life in Christ will never be the same.

May you be loved and blessed by our Father, and may you grow forever deeper in the knowledge of Him who calls you by name.

One Last Vision

Other than editing and working on an appendix, I thought this book was done. You quickly learn when you write a book that done does not mean done; it means kind-of done. I had submitted what I needed to and was happy it was completed. I was finished, but apparently God was not. I had this vision after I was done writing.

At the back of this book is an appendix on hearing God's voice by Mark Virkler. Mark is Charity's father and the President of Communion with God Ministries. He has spent the greater part of his life teaching people around the world the "4 Keys to Hearing God's Voice." I woke up to an email from Mark in which he shared that he had been journaling about the angelic after reading our book. This is the type of impact we are hoping this book has. Here is what Mark heard from the Lord:

> Mark, as you send out legions of angels, to release and accomplish, you will find more than enough coming back in each and every area of your life and ministry. That is My promise to you.
>
> Yes, you set aside angels years ago, as it would have been too controversial, but it is not today. Today is a new day. It is a day to declare angels and their work and service to you. It is the day of the Lord concerning the release of My angels worldwide. It is a NEW DAY. Treat it as a new day and dispatch My legions of angels around the world to accomplish My work and bring healing and restoration to My people.

As I was reading these lines, I had a vision of the heavenly places that was very exciting and encouraging to me. For years, I have battled through a lot of spiritual warfare and become more acquainted with spiritual darkness than I would care to know. This vision was different though. I saw the heavenly places becoming much more active, and the activity was bright and organic. The Lord showed me that this is the angelic. For so long, the second heaven has been filled with darkness. Instead of seeing darkness and evil, I saw the heavens illuminated with brilliant and beautiful colors. It was wonderful to behold. I realized this change in color was due to angels.

You see, the Cross has given the Church unlimited potential through Christ. This is, however, an unrealized potential. We still seem to lose as many battles as we win. This can change. For a long time, God has spoken to me about the end of the age. I do not claim to know exact times and dates, but what I do know is that it will wrap up with unfiltered, unquestioned, supernatural acts of God. This will include angelic activity. The Church is to "make known to the rulers and authorities in the heavenly places the manifold wisdom of God" (Eph. 3:10).

This is what the Lord showed me through the vision after I read Mark's journal entry. Remember, you are the Church and I am the Church. When we walk in divine unity and yielded obedience to Jesus, the demons that occupy the heavenly places will behold the true extent of our salvation—the glorious and triumphant Church! With all my heart I believe angels play a greater role in this than anyone would have expected.

Mark's journal entry was about releasing the angelic. I saw what would happen if not just a few Christians, but a few million Christians, ALL released their angels as God led them. I began to see what the heavens would look like if we did this.

The Bible says that now the god of this age has a level of control. How do we continue to advance? Through Spirit-led fighting. As the Church accepts who she is and embraces her calling to commission the angels God has entrusted to her, I believe this will have a world-changing impact. How would this affect nations, local churches, and our ability to heal and bring deliverance? What would happen if there were ten times as many angels released and active as there were demons?

This is the part we can play as believers. As we grow in our understanding of the angelic, and learn how to corporately release them, the heavenly places will be saturated with more actively engaged angels. As this happens, the strongholds will grow weaker enabling the Church to fight and win with increasingly less resistance. This is the part we will play as we learn to release our everyday angels.

The freedom over us in the heavens will be unlike anything we have known. The angels are not a spiritual luxury God has given us but a dynamic part of His eternal plan. Without partnering with the angelic we will lose battles we are supposed to win. We need our everyday angels, and they need us to assign them to accomplish what they are intended to.

We want this book to be a good education but also a great motivator. We want this book to act as a catalyst to move you into a deeper walk with Christ, where He can teach you about your angels and their role in your life. As more and more Christians understand this and give their angels their assignments, the presence and glory of God will flood the heavenly places, the Church, and indeed the whole earth.

Epilogue

~~The End~~
Just the Beginning!

by Charity Kayembe

As we were finalizing this manuscript on everyday angels, the same weekend Joe had his vision, I too received a glimpse into God's heart for this book's message and how He wants to use it. Joe had a vision during the day, and I had a vision at night—a dream. My dream revealed the stepping-stone to get us to that magnificent goal of increased angelic activity and outpouring of glory.

If we act on my dream, it really will come true.

In the dream, I was in a very busy office building. Both a high-powered businessman with an expensive suit and a young child in simple play clothes (who just seemed to be wandering about) told me they needed to charge their cell phones and asked if I could help.

I had just left my brother Josh down in the parking garage. I told them they should take the elevator down to the parking garage, find him, and they could charge their phones in his car. I said, "Josh is close to the elevator doors, so when you get off the elevator, just call out his name and he will hear and answer you."

I wondered when I'd left my brother why he was sitting in the car with the engine still on. He wasn't going anywhere; he was just waiting with the engine running. I realized though that that worked out great for the people who needed a re-charge. The car was already turned on and ready for them when they got there.

Unpacking the Dream

Most dreams are symbolic. In this dream, the office building represents each one of us. We are usually in the loud and busy offices of our minds, rushing and working and doing.

A cell phone can represent communication. Symbols are personal to the dreamer though, and to me a cell phone specifically represents communication with the spiritual world. When we connect with the supernatural, we are interacting with spirits who aren't "here" and are not visible with our natural eyes. Just like when we talk to someone on the phone, we are having a conversation with someone who isn't here and we can't see.

Two people wanted to charge their cellphones, which means to me that they wanted to reconnect and empower their spiritual interaction. These people represent you. You have just finished reading a book on how to experience the angelic, which demonstrates your desire to connect with the supernatural and empower your communication and engagement with that realm.

The extreme disparity between the focused businessperson with a commanding presence and the distracted child I barely noticed is encouraging because together, they represent everyone. Young and old, analysts and creatives, experts and novices and everyone in between. Together, these two people symbolized the full spectrum of everyone in all walks of life. This definitely includes you, and those two people in the dream represent every potential reader of this book. They represent you!

I was able to help by directing them to the elevator down to the parking garage. That symbolizes how we need to move out of our busy heads and go "down" into our hearts and our spirits in order to make the connection we seek. The elevator moving between floors represents the various heart connection tools we explored (e.g., soaking music, meditation, praying in tongues).

A parking garage can represent a place of rest, because cars are not actively driving. They are still. So we move from our heads, down the elevator to our hearts, into a quiet place of rest and stillness (see Ps. 46:10).

Road Trip with Jesus

There, you meet my brother, Josh. Since his name is Joshua, the English form of *Yeshua*, he's a great dream symbol for our elder Brother, Jesus. I told the businessman and the child to get off the elevator and just call out for him, because he was nearby and would hear them. So you simply have to go down into that place of rest in your heart and Jesus is right there waiting for you. He's so close that you just call His name and He will answer you!

The best part of the dream is that He left the car running. He's waiting for you. Jesus knew what you needed before you even asked, and He already has it ready for you.

Whoever wanted to charge their cellphone was able to plug in. The message of this night vision is that everyone who desires a connection to the sacred supernatural can have it. We are empowered to communicate and interact with the company of Heaven who lives there. It is available!

Just like in the dream, I have given you the directions, the steps to take to get "in spirit" and go down the elevator to the parking garage of your heart. In that place of rest, you will find that Jesus is already waiting for you. You just call to Him and He will answer you. He has what you need: the final symbol of His car represents the vehicle you need for connecting.

God's heart is revealed through this dream as He encourages you to fellowship with Jesus in that quiet place in your spirit and allow His power source to meet your deepest needs and greatest desires. Your desire for supernatural connection and hunger for spiritual encounter delight Him. He is ready to empower you.

Spiritual Four-Minute Mile

No one thought it was possible to run a mile in under four minutes, until Roger Bannister did it. Then, people everywhere were inspired because they knew it was possible, so they went out and ran a four-minute mile, too.

Now you know what's possible with the angelic realm. Now you know that others have interacted with their angels, which means you can do it too. Not only is it possible, it is your inheritance and birthright. You have been born of the Spirit to engage the supernatural. You are called to live and walk by the Spirit!

The Kingdom of Heaven is here, and the Kingdom of Heaven is now. It is a Kingdom filled with God's presence and filled with His holy angels. They are all waiting for you, and it is their great pleasure to show you around. Just like John in the book of Revelation, explore the spirit realm. Let the company of Heaven give you a tour and share their world with you.

Step into the supernatural life you were created for—partnering with God and His angels.

They are ready. The only question is... are you?

Appendix A

How to Be Born of the Spirit

by Dr. Mark Virkler

The Bible says...

1. "The **kingdom of God** is at hand; **Repent** and believe in the gospel" (Mark 1:15).

2. "If you **confess** with your mouth, 'Jesus is Lord,' and **believe** in your heart that God raised Him from the dead, you will be saved" (Romans 10:9).

3. "To all who **received Him**, to those who believed in His name, He gave the right to become children of God" (John 1:11,12).

4. "You will **receive the gift of the Holy Spirit**" (Acts 2:38). "If the Spirit of Him who raised Jesus from the dead dwells in you, He who raised Christ Jesus

from the dead will also give life to your mortal bodies through His Spirit who indwells you" (Romans 8:11).

With a passionate heart and believing mind I pray aloud...

1. *God, I repent for being the ruler of my life and building my own kingdom.*

2. *I confess with my mouth that Jesus is Lord and believe in my heart that God raised Him from the dead.*

3. *I receive You, Jesus, as MY personal Lord, King, Commander and Savior.*

4. *I welcome You, Holy Spirit, into my life to rescue and empower me and restore me to intimacy with my heavenly Father.*

I experience Holy Spirit as I expectantly pray the following...

"God, as I look with the eyes of my heart, show me what is happening." As you tune to His vision (flowing pictures) you may see a picture of Holy Spirit swirling around you and entering you. "Lord, thank You for giving me Your Holy Spirit. Thank You for Your Kingdom emotions of peace, joy, love and hope that are sweeping over me."

"God, I listen with my spiritual ears to what You want to speak to me." As you tune to His voice (flowing thoughts) you are likely to hear Him saying, "I love you, I forgive you. I welcome you home! I'm excited to do life together with you."

"God, what guidance do You want to give me?" Tune to His voice, most often sensed as flowing thoughts, and record what He says in a journal and act on it. Do this daily.

To learn more about your brand new life with Holy Spirit, we invite you to visit www.BornOfTheSpirit.Today.

How to Hear God's Voice

by Dr. Mark Virkler

She had done it again! Instead of coming straight home from school like she was supposed to, she had gone to her friend's house. Without permission. Without our knowledge. Without doing her chores.

With a ministering household that included remnants of three struggling families plus our own toddler and newborn, my wife simply couldn't handle all the work on her own. Everyone had to pull their own weight. Everyone had age-appropriate tasks they were expected to complete. At fourteen, Rachel and her younger brother were living with us while her parents tried to overcome lifestyle patterns that had resulted in the children running away to escape the dysfunction. I felt sorry for Rachel, but, honestly my wife was my greatest concern.

Now Rachel had ditched her chores to spend time with her friends. It wasn't the first time, but if I had anything to say about it, it would be the last. I intended to lay down the law when she got home and make it very clear that if she was going to live under my roof, she would obey my rules.

But...she wasn't home yet. And I had recently been learning to hear God's voice more clearly. Maybe I should try to see if I could hear anything from Him about the situation. Maybe He could give me a way to get her to do what she was supposed to (i.e. what I wanted her to do). So I went to my office and reviewed what the Lord had been teaching me from Habakkuk 2:1-2:

> *I will stand on my guard post and station myself on the rampart; And I will keep watch to see what He will speak to me...Then the Lord answered me and said, "Record the vision...."* (NKJV)

Habakkuk said, "I will stand on my guard post..." (Hab. 2:1). **The first key to hearing God's voice is to go to a quiet place and still our own thoughts and emotions.** Psalm 46:10 encourages us to be still, let go, cease striving, and know that He is God. In Psalm 37:7, we are called to "be still before the Lord and wait patiently for Him." There is a deep inner knowing in our spirits that each of us can experience when we quiet our flesh and our minds. Practicing the art of biblical meditation helps silence the outer noise and distractions clamoring for our attention.

I didn't have a guard post but I did have an office, so I went there to quiet my temper and my mind. Loving God through a quiet worship song is one very effective way to become still. In 2 Kings 3, Elisha needed a word from the Lord so he said, "Bring me a minstrel," and as the minstrel played, the Lord spoke. I have found that playing a worship song on my autoharp is the quickest way for me to come to stillness. I need to choose my song carefully; boisterous songs of praise do not bring me to stillness the way that gentle songs that express my love and worship do. And it isn't enough just to sing the song into the cosmos—I come into the Lord's presence most quickly and easily when I use my godly imagination to see the truth that He is right here with me, and I sing my songs to Him, personally.

"I will keep watch to see," said the prophet. To receive the pure word of God, it is very important that my heart be properly focused as I become still, because my focus is the source of the intuitive flow. If I fix my eyes upon Jesus (see Heb. 12:2), the intuitive flow comes from Jesus. But if I fix my gaze upon some desire of my heart, the intuitive flow comes out of that desire. To have a pure flow, I must become still and carefully fix my eyes upon Jesus. Quietly worshiping the King and receiving out of the stillness that follows quite easily accomplishes this.

So I used **the second key to hearing God's voice: As you pray, fix the eyes of your heart upon Jesus, seeing in the Spirit the dreams and visions of Almighty God.** Habakkuk was actually looking for vision as he prayed. He opened the eyes of his heart and looked into the spirit world to see what God wanted to show him.

God has always spoken through dreams and visions, and He specifically said that they would come to those upon whom the Holy Spirit is poured out (see Acts 2:1-4, 17).

Being a logical, rational person, observable facts that could be verified by my physical senses were the foundations of my life, including my spiritual life. I had never thought of opening the eyes of my heart and looking for vision. However, I have come to believe that this is exactly what God wants me to do. He gave me eyes in my heart to see in the spirit the vision and movement of Almighty God. There is an active spirit world all around us, full of angels, demons, the Holy Spirit, the omnipresent Father, and His omnipresent Son, Jesus. The only reasons for me not to see this reality are unbelief or lack of knowledge.

In his sermon in Acts 2:25, Peter refers to King David's statement: "I saw the Lord always in my presence; for He is at my right hand, so that I will not be shaken." The original psalm makes it clear that this was a decision of David's, not a constant supernatural visitation: "I have set (literally, I have placed) the Lord continually before me; because He is at my right hand, I will not be shaken" (Ps.16:8). Because David knew that the Lord was always with him, he determined in his spirit to see that truth with the eyes of his heart as he went through life, knowing that this would keep his faith strong.

In order to see, we must look. Daniel saw a vision in his mind and said, "I was looking...I kept looking...I kept looking" (Dan. 7:2,9,13). As I pray, I look for Jesus, and I watch as He speaks to me, doing and saying the things that are on His heart. Many Christians will find that if they will only look, they will see. Jesus is Emmanuel, God with us (see Matt. 1:23). It is as simple as that. You can *see* Christ present with you because Christ *is* present with you. In fact, the vision may come so easily that you will be tempted to reject it, thinking that it is just you. But if you persist in recording these visions, your doubt will soon be overcome by faith as you recognize that the content of them could only be birthed in Almighty God.

Jesus demonstrated the ability of living out of constant contact with God, declaring that He did nothing on His own initiative, but only what He saw the Father doing, and heard the Father saying (see John 5:19-20, 30). What an incredible way to live!

Is it possible for us to live out of divine initiative as Jesus did? Yes! We must simply fix our eyes upon Jesus. The veil has been torn, giving access into the immediate presence of God, and He calls us to draw near (see Luke 23:45; Heb. 10:19-22). "I pray that the eyes of your heart will be enlightened..." (Eph. 1:18).

When I had quieted my heart enough that I was able to picture Jesus without the distractions of my own ideas and plans, I was able to "keep watch to see what He will speak to me." I wrote down my question: "Lord, what should I do about Rachel?"

Immediately the thought came to me, "She is insecure." Well, that certainly was not my thought! Her behavior looked like rebellion to me, not insecurity.

But like Habakkuk, I was coming to know the sound of God speaking to me (see Hab. 2:2). Elijah described it as a still, small voice (see I Kings 19:12). I had previously listened for an inner audible voice, and God does speak that way at times. However, I have found that usually, God's voice comes as spontaneous thoughts, visions, feelings, or impressions.

For example, haven't you been driving down the road and had a thought come to you to pray for a certain person? Didn't you believe it was God telling you to pray? What did God's voice sound like? Was it an audible voice, or was it a spontaneous thought that lit upon your mind?

Experience indicates that we perceive spirit-level communication as spontaneous thoughts, impressions, and visions, and Scripture confirms this in many ways. For example, one definition of *paga*, a Hebrew word for intercession, is "a chance encounter or an accidental intersecting." When God lays people on our hearts, He does it through *paga*, a chance-encounter thought "accidentally" intersecting our minds.

So **the third key to hearing God's voice is recognizing that God's voice in your heart often sounds like a flow of spontaneous thoughts.** Therefore, when I want to hear from God, I tune to chance-encounter or spontaneous thoughts.

Finally, God told Habakkuk to record the vision (Hab. 2:2). This was not an isolated command. The Scriptures record many examples of individual's prayers and God's replies, such as the Psalms, many of the prophets, and Revelation. I have found that obeying this final principle has amplified my confidence in my ability to hear God's voice so that I could finally make living out of His initiatives a way of life. **The fourth key, two-way journaling or the writing out of your prayers and God's answers, brings great freedom in hearing God's voice.**

I have found two-way journaling to be a fabulous catalyst for clearly discerning God's inner, spontaneous flow, because as I journal I am able to write in faith for long periods of time, simply believing it is God. I know that what I believe I have received from God must be tested. However, testing involves doubt and doubt blocks divine communication, so I do not want to test while I am trying to receive (see James 1:5-8). With journaling, I can receive in faith, knowing that when the flow has ended I can test and examine it carefully.

I wrote down what I believed He had said: "She is insecure."

But the Lord wasn't done. I continued to write the spontaneous thoughts that came to me: "Love her unconditionally. She is flesh of your flesh and bone of your bone."

My mind immediately objected: She is not flesh of my flesh. She is not related to me at all— she is a foster child, just living in my home temporarily. It was definitely time to test this "word from the Lord"!

There are three possible sources of thoughts in our minds: ourselves, satan, and the Holy Spirit. It was obvious that the words in my journal did not come from my own mind—I certainly didn't see her as insecure or flesh of my flesh. And I sincerely doubted that satan would encourage me to love anyone unconditionally!

Okay, it was starting to look like I might have actually received counsel from the Lord. It was consistent with the names and character of God as revealed in the Scripture, and totally contrary to the names and character of the enemy. So that meant that I was hearing from the Lord, and He wanted me to see the situation in a different light. Rachel was my daughter—part of my family, not by blood but by the hand of God Himself. The chaos of her birth home had created deep insecurity about her worthiness to be loved by anyone, including me and including God. Only the unconditional love of the Lord expressed through an imperfect human would reach her heart.

But there was still one more test I needed to perform before I would have absolute confidence that this was truly God's word to me: I needed confirmation from someone else whose spiritual discernment I trusted. So I went to my wife and shared what I had received. I knew if I could get her validation, especially since she was the one most wronged in the situation, then I could say, at least to myself, "Thus sayeth the Lord."

Needless to say, Patti immediately and without question confirmed that the Lord had spoken to me. My entire planned lecture was forgotten. I returned to my office anxious to hear more. As the Lord planted a new, supernatural love for Rachel within me, He showed me what to say and how to say it to not only address the current issue of household responsibility, but the deeper issues of love and acceptance and worthiness.

Rachel and her brother remained as part of our family for another two years, giving us many opportunities to demonstrate and teach about the Father's love, planting spiritual seeds in thirsty soil. We weren't perfect and we didn't solve all of her issues, but because I had learned to listen to the Lord, we were able to avoid creating more brokenness and separation.

The four simple keys that the Lord showed me from Habakkuk have been used by people of all ages, from four to ninety-four, from every continent, culture and denomination, to break through into intimate two-way conversations with their loving Father and dearest Friend. Omitting any one of the keys will prevent you from receiving all He wants to say to you. The order of the keys is not important, just that you use them all. Embracing all four, by faith, can change your life. Simply quiet yourself down, tune to spontaneity, look for vision, and journal. He is waiting to meet you there.

You will be amazed when you journal! Doubt may hinder you at first, but throw it off, reminding yourself that it is a biblical concept, and that God is present, speaking to His children. Relax. When we cease our labors and enter His rest, God is free to flow (see Heb. 4:10).

Why not try it for yourself, right now? Sit back comfortably, take out your pen and paper, and smile. Turn your attention toward the Lord in praise and worship, seeking His face. Many people have found the music and visionary prayer called "A Stroll Along the Sea of Galilee" helpful in getting them started. You can listen to it and download it free at www.CWGMinistries.org/Galilee.

After you write your question to Him, become still, fixing your gaze on Jesus. You will suddenly have a very good thought. Don't doubt it; simply write it down. Later, as you read your journaling, you, too, will be blessed to discover that you are indeed dialoguing with God. If you wonder if it is really the Lord speaking to you, share it with your spouse or a friend. Their input will encourage your faith and strengthen your commitment to spend time getting to know the Lover of your soul more intimately than you ever dreamed possible.

Is It *Really* God?

Five ways to be sure what you are hearing is from Him:

1) *Test the Origin (see 1 John 4:1)*

Thoughts from our own minds are progressive, with one thought leading to the next, however tangentially. Thoughts from the spirit world are spontaneous. The Hebrew word for true prophecy is *naba*, which literally means to bubble up, whereas false prophecy is *ziyd* meaning to boil up. True words from the Lord will bubble up from our innermost being; we don't need to cook them up ourselves.

2) *Compare It to Biblical Principles*

God will never say something to you personally which is contrary to His universal revelation as expressed in the Scriptures. If the Bible clearly states that something is a sin, no amount of journaling can make it right. Much of what you journal about, however, will not be specifically addressed in the Bible, so an understanding of biblical principles is also needed.

3) *Compare It to the Names and Character of God as Revealed in the Bible*

Anything God says to you will be in harmony with His essential nature. Journaling will help you get to know God personally, but knowing what the Bible says about Him will help you discern what words are from Him. Make sure the tenor of your journaling lines up with the character of God as described in the names of the Father, Son and Holy Spirit.

4) *Test the Fruit (see Matt. 7:15-20)*

What effect does what you are hearing have on your soul and your spirit? Words from the Lord will quicken your faith and increase your love, peace, and joy. They will stimulate a sense of humility within you as you become more aware of Who God is and who you are. On the other hand, any words you receive which cause you to fear or doubt, which bring you into confusion or anxiety, or which stroke your ego (especially if you hear something that is "just for you alone— no one else is worthy") must be immediately rebuked and rejected as lies of the enemy.

5) Share It with Your Spiritual Counselors (see Prov. 11:14)

We are members of a Body! A cord of three strands is not easily broken and God's intention has always been for us to grow together. Nothing will increase your faith in your ability to hear from God like having it confirmed by two or three other people! Share it with your spouse, your parents, your friends, your elder, your group leader, even your grown children can be your sounding board. They don't need to be perfect or super-spiritual; they just need to love you, be committed to being available to you, have a solid biblical orientation, and most importantly, they must also willingly and easily receive counsel. Avoid the authoritarian who insists that because of their standing in the church or with God, they no longer need to listen to others. Find two or three people and let them confirm that you are hearing from God!

Book and training resources on 4 Keys to Hearing God's Voice are available at www.CWGMinistries.org.

Does the Bible Talk About Angels? 365 Scriptural References

Compiled by Joe Brock

This appendix lists all the verses that make reference to the angelic in the New American Standard Bible (1977 ed.). We have included verses with the word *Angel, Cherub(im), and Seraphim*. As you can see, Scripture is saturated with references to these heavenly beings.

Angel (including Angels, Angel's, Angelic) — 295 references

Some verses have the word "angel" in it more than once. We have only included the verse one time.

Gen 16:7	Gen 16:11	Gen 21:17	Gen 24:7
Gen 16:9	Gen 19:1	Gen 22:11	Gen 24:40
Gen 16:10	Gen 19:15	Gen 22:15	Gen 28:12

Gen 31:11	Judg 13:18	Isa 63:9	Matt 16:27
Gen 32:1	Judg 13:20	Dan 3:28	Matt 18:10
Gen 48:16	Judg 13:21	Dan 4:13*	Matt 22:30
Ex 3:2	1 Sam 29:9	Dan 4:17*	Matt 24:31
Ex 14:19	2 Sam 14:17	Dan 4:23*	Matt 24:36
Ex 23:20	2 Sam 14:20	Dan 6:22	Matt 25:31
Ex 23:23	2 Sam 19:27	Hos 12:4	Matt 25:41
Ex 32:34	2 Sam 24:16	Zech 1:9	Matt 26:53
Ex 33:2	2 Sam 24:16	Zech 1:11	Matt 28:2
Num 20:16	2 Sam 24:17	Zech 1:12	Matt 28:5
Num 22:22	1 Kings 13:18	Zech 1:13	Mark 1:13
Num 22:23	1 Kings 19:5	Zech 1:14	Mark 8:38
Num 22:24	1 Kings 19:7	Zech 1:19	Mark 12:25
Num 22:25	2 Kings 1:3	Zech 2:3	Mark 13:27
Num 22:26	2 Kings 1:15	Zech 3:1	Mark 13:32
Num 22:27	2 Kings 19:35	Zech 3:3	Luke 1:11
Num 22:31	1 Chron 21:12	Zech 3:5	Luke 1:13
Num 22:32	1 Chron 21:15	Zech 3:6	Luke 1:18
Num 22:34	1 Chron 21:16	Zech 4:1	Luke 1:19
Num 22:35	1 Chron 21:18	Zech 4:4	Luke 1:26
Judg 2:1	1 Chron 21:20	Zech 4:5	Luke 1:30
Judg 2:4	1 Chron 21:27	Zech 5:5	Luke 1:34
Judg 5:23	1 Chron 21:30	Zech 5:10	Luke 1:35
Judg 6:11	2 Chron 32:21	Zech 6:4	Luke 1:38
Judg 6:12	Job 4:18	Zech 6:5	Luke 2:9
Judg 6:20	Job 33:23	Zech 12:8	Luke 2:10
Judg 6:21	Ps 34:7	Matt 1:20	Luke 2:13
Judg 6:22	Ps 35:5	Matt 1:24	Luke 2:15
Judg 13:3	Ps 35:6	Matt 2:13	Luke 2:21
Judg 13:6	Ps 78:25	Matt 2:19	Luke 4:10
Judg 13:9	Ps 78:49	Matt 4:6	Luke 9:26
Judg 13:13	Ps 91:11	Matt 4:11	Luke 12:8
Judg 13:15	Ps 103:20	Matt 13:39	Luke 12:9
Judg 13:16	Ps 148:2	Matt 13:41	Luke 15:10
Judg 13:17	Isa 37:36	Matt 13:49	Luke 16:22

Luke 20:36	2 Cor 11:14	Rev 3:1	Rev 14:8
Luke 22:43	Gal 1:8	Rev 3:5	Rev 14:9
Luke 24:23	Gal 3:19	Rev 3:7	Rev 14:10
John 1:51	Gal 4:14	Rev 3:14	Rev 14:15
John 5:4	Col 2:18	Rev 5:2	Rev 14:17
John 12:29	2 Thess 1:7	Rev 5:11	Rev 14:18
John 20:12	1 Tim 3:16	Rev 7:1	Rev 14:19
Acts 5:19	1 Tim 5:21	Rev 7:2	Rev 15:1
Acts 6:15	Heb 1:4	Rev 7:11	Rev 15:6
Acts 7:30	Heb 1:5	Rev 8:2	Rev 15:7
Acts 7:35	Heb 1:6	Rev 8:3	Rev 15:8
Acts 7:38	Heb 1:7	Rev 8:4	Rev 16:1
Acts 7:53	Heb 1:13	Rev 8:5	Rev 16:2*
Acts 8:26	Heb 2:2	Rev 8:6	Rev 16:3*
Acts 10:3	Heb 2:5	Rev 8:8	Rev 16:4*
Acts 10:7	Heb 2:7	Rev 8:10	Rev 16:5
Acts 10:22	Heb 2:9	Rev 8:12	Rev 16:8*
Acts 11:13	Heb 2:16	Rev 8:13	Rev 16:10*
Acts 12:7	Heb 12:22	Rev 9:1	Rev 16:12*
Acts 12:8	Heb 13:2	Rev 9:11	Rev 16:17*
Acts 12:9	1 Peter 1:12	Rev 9:13	Rev 17:1
Acts 12:10	1 Peter 3:22	Rev 9:14	Rev 17:7
Acts 12:11	2 Peter 2:4	Rev 9:15	Rev 18:1
Acts 12:15	2 Peter 2:10	Rev 10:1	Rev 18:21
Acts 12:23	2 Peter 2:11	Rev 10:5	Rev 19:17
Acts 23:8	Jude 6	Rev 10:7	Rev 20:1
Acts 23:9	Jude 8	Rev 10:8	Rev 21:9
Acts 27:23	Rev 1:1	Rev 10:9	Rev 21:12
Rom 8:38	Rev 1:20	Rev 10:10	Rev 21:17
1 Cor 4:9	Rev 2:1	Rev 11:15	Rev 22:6
1 Cor 6:3	Rev 2:8	Rev 12:7	Rev 22:8
1 Cor 11:10	Rev 2:12	Rev 12:9	Rev 22:16
1 Cor 13:1	Rev 2:18	Rev 14:6	

* These references have the word "angel" in the NASB but not in the original languages. The word was added to clarify the meaning.

Cherub/Cherubim — 68 References

Some verses have "Cherub/Cherubim" in it more than once. We have only listed these verses one time.

Gen 3:24	1 Kings 6:25	2 Chron 3:13	Ezek 10:8
Ex 25:18	1 Kings 6:26	2 Chron 3:14	Ezek 10:9
Ex 25:19	1 Kings 6:27	2 Chron 5:7	Ezek 10:14
Ex 25:20	1 Kings 6:28	2 Chron 5:8	Ezek 10:15
Ex 25:22	1 Kings 6:29	Ezra 2:59	Ezek 10:16
Ex 26:1	1 Kings 6:32	Neh 7:61	Ezek 10:17
Ex 26:31	1 Kings 6:35	Ps 18:10	Ezek 10:18
Ex 36:8	1 Kings 7:29	Ps 80:1	Ezek 10:19
Ex 36:35	1 Kings 7:36	Ps 99:1	Ezek 10:20
Ex 37:7	1 Kings 8:6	Isa 37:16	Ezek 11:22
Ex 37:8	1 Kings 8:7	Ezek 9:3	Ezek 28:14
Ex 37:9	2 Kings 19:15	Ezek 10:1	Ezek 28:16
Num 7:89	1 Chron 13:6	Ezek 10:2	Ezek 41:18
1 Sam 4:4	1 Chron 28:18	Ezek 10:3	Ezek 41:20
2 Sam 6:2	2 Chron 3:7	Ezek 10:4	Ezek 41:25
2 Sam 22:11	2 Chron 3:10	Ezek 10:5	Heb 9:5
1 Kings 6:23	2 Chron 3:11	Ezek 10:6	
1 Kings 6:24	2 Chron 3:12	Ezek 10:7	

Seraphim—2 References

Isaiah 6:2	Isaiah 6:6

Endnotes

1. Bill Johnson, *Hosting the Presence* (Shippensburg, PA: Destiny Image, 2012), 103-104.

2. Mohd. Razali Salleh, "Advances in Pediatrics," October 2008, https://www.ncbi.nlm.nih.gov/pmc/articles/PMC3341916/.

3. To learn more about the miraculous benefits of living from God's heart, check out our training on Unleashing Healing Power Through Spirit-Born Emotions. Once my angels got us started on this journey to our happy place, the Kingdom within, my Dad and I discovered so many scientific studies and Scripture to back up the revelation, we had to write a whole book about it! (www.GloryWaves.org/products)

4. Marie Chapian, *Angels in Our Lives* (Shippensburg: Destiny Image, 2016), Kindle 255.

5. Mark Virkler and Charity Virkler Kayembe, *Hearing God Through Your Dreams,* (Shippensburg: Destiny Image, 2016).

6. "Discerning Angels and Other Heavenly Beings" video, Patricia King Institute, produced 2016 by XP Media, Maricopa, AZ.

7. C. Fred Dickason, *Angels: Elect & Evil* (Chicago, IL: Moody Publishers, 1995), 27.

8. Georgian Banov, qtd. in Jonathan Dixon, *Angel Stories,* (Lake Mary, FL: Charisma House, 2014), 182.

9. Dr. Tim Sheets, *Angel Armies: Releasing the Warriors of Heaven,* (Shippensburg: Destiny Image, 2016), 150, 153.

10. Dr. Tim Sheets, *Angel Armies: Releasing the Warriors of Heaven,* (Shippensburg: Destiny Image, 2016), 53-54.

11. Bill Johnson, *When Heaven Invades Earth,* (Shippensburg: Destiny Image, 2003), 141.

12. David Herzog, qtd. in Jonathan Dixon, *Angel Stories,* (Lake Mary, FL: Charisma House, 2014), 39-40.

13. Bobby Connor, *Heaven's Host: The Assignments of Angels Both Faithful and Fallen* (Bullard, TX: EaglesView Ministries, 2013), 100.

14. Jamie Galloway, *Secrets of the Seer,* (Shippensburg: Destiny Image, 2017), 50.

15. www.CWGMinistries.org/4Keys

16. If you don't know Jesus, He'd love to meet you! You are welcome to learn more in Appendix A and pray through this site: www.BornOfTheSpirit.Today.

17. To learn more about your spiritual senses, refer to the 4 Keys to Hearing God's Voice resources at www.CWGMinistries.org/4Keys.

18. www.cwgministries.org/store/empowered-spirit-complete-package and there are two free videos here www.cwgministries.org/tonguesvideo

19. Quantum physics demonstrates that 99.9999% of atoms are empty space and that matter only appears solid. In reality, it is mostly energy. An article that explains this phenomenon in an easy-to-understand way is available to review here: www.sciencealert.com/99-9999999-of-your-body-is-empty-space.

20. www.cwgministries.org/blogs/perfect-peace-when-your
    -imagination

21. Patricia King, *Eyes That See,* (Maricopa, AZ: XP Publishing, 2010), 63.

22. Katie Souza, qtd. in Jonathan Dixon, *Angel Stories,* (Lake Mary, FL: Charisma House, 2014), 65.

23. Jim Richards, *Moving Your Invisible Boundaries,* (Travelers Rest: True Potential, 2013), 16.

24. Mark Virkler and Charity Virkler Kayembe, *Unleashing Healing Power Through Spirit-Born Emotions,* (Shippensburg: Destiny Image, 2017).

25 CWGMinistries.org/SpiritualTransformations

26. To learn more, visit www.glorywaves.org/eft.

27. Charity Virkler Kayembe and Sherrie Rice Smith, *EFT for Christians: Tapping into God's Peace and Joy* (Travelers Rest, SC: True Potential Publishing, 2016).

28. Biblically-Based EFT training resources, co-taught with Dr. Jim Richards available at www.GloryWaves.org/products (Huntsville, AL: Impact Ministries, 2016).

29. www.GloryWaves.org/Angels

30. www.glorywaves.org/quantum

31. Emily Dickinson, *The Poems of Emily Dickinson* (Edited by R. W. Franklin) (Cambridge: Harvard University Press, 1999), "Forever— is composed of Nows."

32. Quora, "Einstein Believed In A Theory Of Spacetime That Can Help People Cope With Loss," Forbes, December 28, 2016, https://www.forbes.com/sites/quora/2016/12/28/einstein-believed-in-a-theory-of-spacetime-that-can-help-people-cope-with-loss/#77538de955d2.

33. *How to Walk by the Spirit* book, CDs and DVDs by Mark and Patti Virkler available at www.cwgministries.org.

34. Phil Mason, *Quantum Glory: The Science of Heaven Invading Earth,* (Maricopa, AZ: XP Publishing, 2010), 77.

35. Dawson Church, *The Genie in Your Genes: Epigenetic Medicine and the New Biology of Intention,* (Fulton, Energy Psychology Press, 2014), 208.

36. All testimonies used with permission.

37. Marie Chapian, *Angels in Our Lives,* (Shippensburg: Destiny Image, 2006), Kindle 251.

38. Bobby Connor, *Heaven's Host: The Assignments of Angels Both Faithful and Fallen* (Bullard, TX: EaglesView Ministries, 2013), 45-46.

About the Authors

CHARITY VIRKLER KAYEMBE is passionate about the sacred supernatural and making the mystical practical in believers' everyday lives. She has been featured on Sid Roth's *It's Supernatural!*, Cornerstone TV, Charisma Magazine and The Elijah List. Charity has a Doctorate in Biblical Studies and writes about the unfolding adventure that is walking by the Spirit on her blog at GloryWaves.org. Her international outreach has taken her to all corners of the globe, traveling to over 60 nations on six continents. She and her husband live in upstate New York.

JOE BROCK has nearly 25 years in pastoral, prophetic, and deliverance ministry. He has a B.A. in Christian Ministries (Bethel College, IN) and is currently working towards a Th.D. through Christian Leadership University. Joe began encountering the angelic around 10 years ago and has seen their involvement in his life increase steadily. It is Joe's truest desire to help those he can through the transitions of their faith.

Discover More from
Charity Kayembe and Joe Brock

 **Dr. Charity Virkler Kayembe** has developed training resources on the sacred supernatural including an accompanying DVD series on Everyday Angels. With new and different stories plus a time of angelic activation, the videos are designed to be used in conjunction with this book and are perfect for individual or small group use: GloryWaves.org/products

Find **free teaching** and interviews at:
GloryWaves.org/free-media

Check out Charity's **latest angel adventures** and watch her *Angels Q&A* at: **GloryWaves.org/angels**

Learn the basics of how to **translate God's messages** to you while you sleep in her free Dreams Crash Course at:
GloryWaves.org/dreams

Host Charity in your community to speak at your church or event. Details on available training and workshops at:
GloryWaves.org/seminars

She is blogging regularly at **GloryWaves.org/blog** and you can follow her at:
Facebook.com/GloryWavesMinistries
Instagram.com/GloryWavesMinistries
Twitter.com/Glory_Waves

Charity serves as the Vice President of Academic Affairs at **Christian Leadership University**, an online school that puts the voice of God in the center of your learning experience. Discover more at: **CLUOnline.com**

Honor **Holy Spirit's role** in your salvation: **www.BornOfTheSpirit .Today**

 **Joe Brock** is available to conduct seminars on this and other topics and can be reached via email at joebrockministries@gmail.com or by phone at his church office: 765-675-7689. You can find Joe's products for sale at: www.joe-brock5020.myshopify.com

Interactive Online Training from **CLU School of the Spirit**

How Far Could **You** Go with a Bible School in Your Pocket?

Can I really experience a "school of the Spirit" in my home? *Yes, you can!*

- ☑ You don't have to go away to Bible school or a school of ministry.

- ☑ You can live in any city in any country, attend any church, and still earn a Diploma in Applied Spirituality from Christian Leadership University's School of the Spirit! CLU provides *interactive* Spirit Life Training Modules that feature video training experiences and online quizzes, all of which can be downloaded directly to your laptop, tablet, or smart phone.

Don't you think it's time YOU team up and focus with a coach at your side so you speed forward and enter your Promised Land?

There is no easier way to grow than to get into a group of like-minded people and focus intently, under the direction of Holy Spirit and a coach who is ahead of you in the area you are pursuing. *"A cord of three strands is not quickly broken"* (Eccles. 4:12 NIV). You support one another through the training process and by "focusing intently," you become a doer of the Word and not a hearer only (see James 1:25). No one wants to die in their wilderness so make sure you are taking the proper steps that will allow you to experience your Promised Land!

**Learn more and try our
FREE Course Sampler today:
www.CLUSchooloftheSpirit.com**

Everyday Angels
Interactive e-Learning Course

Coaching speeds you to *mastery*

We guarantee you *will* learn how to partner with the angels God assigned to you! We can teach you in just three months what it took us years to learn because we have gone ahead and prepared the way. And these exercises are so spiritual in nature you can easily complete them as part of your daily devotional time.

When you meditate on revelation truths in the context of a CLU School of the Spirit course, you are required to fully integrate the life-changing principles. Nothing is left to chance. You will learn what you are supposed to learn, and your life will be transformed by the power of the Holy Spirit.

Look at ALL you will receive in this interactive Spirit Life Training Module!

- ☑ Entire series of downloadable videos
- ☑ MP3 audio sessions
- ☑ Complete PDF ebook
- ☑ Step-by-step guidance from the Interactive Learning Management System
- ☑ Certificate of Completion awarding 5 CEUs
- ☑ Coaching

Learn more and enroll today at
www.CLUSchooloftheSpirit.com/angels